The Ultimate Unofficial Guide to Minecraft® Strategies

The Ultimate Unofficial Guide to Minecraft® Strategies

Everything You Need to Know to Build, Explore, Attack, and Survive in the World of Minecraft

- -

Instructables.com, Edited by Nicole Smith

Skyhorse Publishing

Skyhorse Publishing books may be purchased in bulk at special discounts for sales promotion, corporate gifts, fund-raising, or educational purposes. Special editions can also be created to specifications. For details, contact the Special Sales Department, Skyhorse Publishing, 307 West 36th Street, 11th Floor, New York, NY 10018 or info@skyhorsepublishing.com.

Skyhorse® and Skyhorse Publishing® are registered trademarks of Skyhorse Publishing, Inc.®, a Delaware corporation.

www.skyhorsepublishing.com

10 9 8 7 6 5 4 3 2 1

Library of Congress Cataloging-in-Publication Data is available on file.

Cover design by Brian Peterson
Cover photo credit: Nicole Smith

Print ISBN: 978-1-63220-241-3
Ebook ISBN: 978-1-63220-249-9

Printed in China

Table of Contents

Introduction

Welcome to the world of Minecraft! Dirt, Sand, Stone and Ore are all pixelated parts of the game which you can collect and re-shape into your own little world. Collect and craft resources to build your hovel into a home, your home into a town, and your town into a fortress! Minecraft is a sandbox construction game with endless possibilities.

You can choose to play creatively with unlimited resources at your fingertips and no monsters to threaten your gameplay, or you can dive head first into survival mode with your fists as your only tool. With survival you are thrown into a whole new world and you don't have much time to get your bearings. Follow along with our tutorials as we show you how to survive your first day and night out on your own. Learn about collecting resources, finding food, and building a shelter to protect you from the hostile mobs that come out at night. Once you've figured out how to stay alive, you can begin to learn about the basics of Minecraft including mining, farming, and raising and breeding animals. After following along with these great Instructables you will be able to move onto creating interesting new structures including a Castle, a Tower, or even an enormous Glass Dome.

Learn about all the different areas and creatures you will encounter as you travel around the never-ending landscapes before you in Minecraft. Once you think you have the world figured out, you can build a Nether Portal and venture into the darker side of Minecraft: The Nether. Filled with fire, lava and monsters who shoot fire, there will be excitement at every turn and you can learn everything you need to know right here to fight the monsters and survive! Be prepared and don't forget to bring along *The Ultimate Unofficial Guide to Minecraft® Strategies* to help you along your way in Minecraft!

—Nicole (Penolopy Bulnick)

Basic Gameplay

How to Survive Your First Day

Nicole Smith

(http://www.instructables.com/id/How-to-Survive-Your-First-Day-in-Minecraft/)

Minecraft is a sandbox construction game where you are thrown into a world in which you need to adapt, explore, and survive. It can be overwhelming and difficult to just jump right in, so this tutorial will give you the basics of how to get started and survive your first day in Minecraft.

Step 1: Generating the World

When you open the game you have a few options to choose from before getting started. I will outline the basics, but there are more that you can explore when you play yourself. The first thing you need to decide is whether you want to play in survival, creative, or hardcore mode.

Survival:

With survival mode, you are thrown into a world and must fend to survive. You can change the difficulty (difficulties are outlined below), and you must gather all the resources you need to survive.

Creative:

You start with everything you could ever find or create in the game (instead of your inventory screen you have a selection screen from which you can pick out anything to use). Instead of needing tools to destroy blocks, you can break anything with one hit. You do not have to worry about eating or a health bar. You cannot die even if you jump off a cliff or walk through lava. Lastly, you can fly!

Hardcore:

This mode is like survival except you are on the hardest difficulty level, which you cannot change. You also only have one life to live. Think of this as real life.

Difficulty Levels for Survival Mode:

- Peaceful: easiest, no monsters, you can still get hurt and die, such as from falling or trying to walk on lava. Your food bar will never deplete, and because of that you cannot eat.
- Easy: hostile mobs will spawn, but do not damage you as much. Also, the cave spiders cannot poison you at this level. You can survive if food meter runs out.
- Normal: hostile mobs spawn and will deal you more damage. In this level, you can still survive if the food meter runs out, but it will run down to half a heart.
- Hard: hostile mobs will spawn and cause you the most damage of all the difficulties. If you let your food meter run all the way down, your health will slowly deplete until you die. While doors will usually keep mobs out, at this level, zombies can break down the wood doors.

FOV:

Another thing you can choose is your FOV (Field of Vision). It ranges from 70° to 110°. 70° is the default and what most people use. You can also change this during gameplay.

Now it's time to generate your world! You never know what it is going to be. It could be a flat desert with nothing for miles, you could immediately be left on an island surrounded by water, or you could get a perfect world with trees and caves aplenty. You will have to adapt to your surroundings right away. Also, make sure to watch your step or you could fall into a cave right away! If you are lucky, you will just take damage, but you could die or you could be stuck in a hole with no light and no supplies to make weapons. So watch your step! Wherever you start is called your spawn point. If you die, you will appear back at this spawn point.

Also, one day in Minecraft = ten minutes of real time, so time to get to work!

Step 2: Wood

The first thing you are going to want to do is to gather wood. It is a necessary resource and you can get it easily by just punching trees (some resources require specific tools to obtain them).

Just start breaking down all the trees you can.

Tip: Sometimes the trees are too tall to break all the blocks from the ground. One thing you can do is skip the first (bottom) block and break the two above it. Then you can stand on that block and look up and continue to break all the blocks of the trunk. When you are done, hop down and break the block you were standing on. If you break all the wood of the tree, the leaves will slowly disappear and can drop saplings for planting and even apples!

If the tree is way too tall, you can create a Nerd Pole. A nerd pole is when you look straight down, jump, and then lay a block down so you can create a pole while standing on it. I suggest you use dirt, as it is easy to re-destroy. To get down, just look down and break the dirt until you are on ground level. (You can also just jump down and leave the dirt if you don't care about it and if you aren't too high that you will get hurt.)

Once you have wood, you can create a crafting table. That is one of the things you can create in your inventory crafting grid (2 x 2). Many things take a crafting station crafting grid to create them.

To make a crafting table, put one piece of wood in, which will create wooden planks. One wood block = four planks.

Use four planks to make a crafting station. Four planks in a square = one crafting table.

Once you have the crafting table, just set it on the ground to use it. Now you can create more complicated things like tools and doors.

Step 3: Shelter

Once you have wood, finding or creating shelter is the next thing to knock off your list.

One of the easiest ways to do this is to find a dirt hill and carve out a hole in it. Dirt is nice because you can easily break it with your hands. You can also go into stone, but you will need to make a pickax first.

Once night falls, you will need to get in your shelter. You have to make sure you are not exposed to the world. Your options are to:

- Block yourself in completely (with wood, dirt, stone, etc.).
- Create a door: six wood planks in two columns side by side = one wood door. Block yourself in except for one 1 x 1 block, which little can fit through. Block yourself in with glass so you can see outside (once glass is placed you can only destroy it; you can't break it and pick it back up). You can smelt sand to get glass.

How to Mine

Nicole Smith

http://www.instructables.com/id/How-to-Mine-in-Minecraft/

There are so many ways to approach mining in Minecraft. I want to cover some of the ways you can get started, whether it is with careful planning or by just jumping right into it!

Step 1: Setting Up a Mining Station

Before you go exploring down into your mines (whatever type of mine they may be), it is a good idea to set up a mining station. What you put it in is up to you, but here are some suggestions and the reasoning behind them. It helps to have one of these at the surface of your mine, but you can have it wherever you want, and you can make more of them as your area of exploration expands.

- Bed—if you die, you will spawn back here instead of somewhere far away.
- Chest—hopefully you will mine many things and you won't be able to hold it all, so having a chest in a safe place is a good way to save your items, especially if you were to die.
- Furnace—so you can smelt the ores you find.
- Crafting table—you will undoubtedly need more tools and other various items while mining, so it is good to have a crafting table nearby.

Step 2: Tools of the Trade

In order to mine you are going to need tools.

Crafting Tools (wood, stone, iron, diamond, and gold)
- 1 Ore + 2 Sticks = Shovel
- 3 Ores + 2 Sticks = Pickax
- 2 Ores + 1 Stick = Sword

Fixing Tools

As you use your tools, they will wear down. The bar indicating the amount of uses left on it will start green and go red when it is about to break. If you take two worn-down tools (of the same material) and craft them together, it will combine their uses they have left. They will take up one place in your inventory instead of two now.

What to Carry with You:
- Pickaxes—you will have to start with a stone pickax, most likely, so carry a couple of them. When you can, start carrying an iron pickax to get those ores that need at least that to be mined.
- Shovel—when you are mining, you probably won't run into dirt or sand, but there can be some, and you are bound to run into gravel, so it can be handy to have a shovel to speed up your digging.
- Sword—as long as you are playing on survival mode, you will run into a hostile mob, and you will need to defend yourself.
- Signs—or some way to mark where you have been. It can get confusing when you explore mines formed in the game, as paths go in all different directions, and it can be hard to find your way back to your mining station or the surface.
- Food—you will need it eventually, so it is good to have some with you and some stored at your station.
- Buckets—they can be stacked, but they will take up their own spaces when filled, so keep that in mind for space; it can be handy to have a bucket of water to put out lava, or an empty bucket to collect that lava.
- Torches—you will need lots of them, as you will need them to see what you are doing and to

prevent mobs from spawning near you; they can also be used as markers to show where you have been or where you are going.

- Dirt—I find it handy to have a stack of dirt on hand, as I use it to get around lava and pits, and also to mark off where I have been; it is nice since it is easy to break and pick back up and it really stands out against the stone.
- Wood—great to have in case you need to build tools, crafting table, torches, etc.

Crafting:

- 6 Wooden Planks + 1 Stick = 3 Signs
- 3 Iron Ingots (in a "U" shape) = 1 Bucket

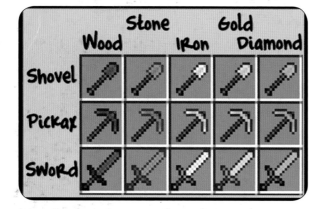

Step 3: Carts and Rails

The more you play the game, the more efficient you can be. Some things you can make that will make mining more efficient are carts and tracks. These start pretty basic and can be souped up to be pretty awesome.

Crafting Minecarts

- 5 Iron Ingots in a "U" = Minecart
- Minecart + Chest = Minecart with Chest
- Minecart + Furnace = Minecart with Furnace
- Minecart + Hopper = Minecart with Hopper
- Minecart + TNT = Minecart with TNT

Crafting Rails

- 6 Iron Ingots + 1 Stick = 16 Rails
- 6 Gold Ingots + 1 Stick + 1 Redstone = 6 Powered Rails
- 6 Iron Ingots + 1 Stone Pressure Plate + 1 Redstone = 6 Detector Rails
- 6 Iron Ingots + 1 Redstone Torch + 2 Sticks = 6 Activator Rails

Step 4: TNT

TNT can be used to help with mining, but you need to keep in mind that it will destroy some of the resources that are released from broken blocks. It is more of an aid in removing large areas quickly and not for actually mining resources. You can light the TNT in different ways, but the most common way is with flint and steel. Some resources are immune to explosions, such as obsidian, and can be used to direct explosions and prevent things from being destroyed. When TNT is ignited, it will jump slightly and then blink white as it counts down to exploding. The delay is only about four seconds, so it is best to run once it's lit.

- 4 Sand Blocks + 5 Pieces of Gunpowder = 1 TNT
- 1 Iron Ingot + 1 Flint = Flint and Steel

Step 5: Cave Mining

The easiest and most common way to mine in the game is by cave mining. It just consists of exploring the world and finding exposed mines and gorges. Then you explore the cave and mine out any exposed ores and resources. Once everything is found, you can move on.

Note: After trying out all of the methods mentioned in this Instructable, this method seems to yield the best results. It takes less time (since you don't have to do as much digging) and you are likely to find a bigger variety of ores.

Step 6: Abandoned Mines

Abandoned mines are great. They are a wealth of resources, and that includes more than just exposed ores; for instance, saddles, which cannot be crafted—they have to be found. In mines you will find:

- Rails—you can collect and place elsewhere.
- Chests—a gold mine of supplies, plus now you have a chest.
- Carts—one less thing to make and you can use them to get around, but be careful, rails are rarely complete in abandoned mines.
- Webs—can be destroyed with a sword to get string.

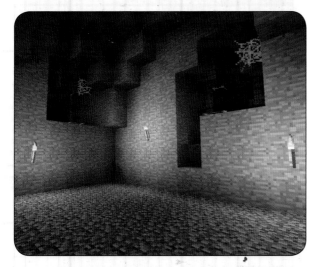

Step 7: Shaft Mining

Shaft mining involves just digging on your own in the pursuit of ores. The main way to shaft mine is to dig a staircase, leaving yourself enough room to jump your way back to the surface. You can also actually place stairs, which are convenient since jumping up blocks takes more energy and with stairs you can just walk back up.

Be careful not to dig straight down, as you can dig into existing caves, receive damage, and possibly fall into lava.

I mentioned stairs, but that isn't the only way to get up and down in a shaft mine. To get back up, you can also craft and use ladders. They are convenient as you only need a 1 x 1 square shaft to get back up. Another way to get back up is to first pour out a bucket of water at the top of a shaft and use that to swim back up when you are at the bottom.

To get down you can use stairs and ladders (both as mentioned) or destroy a block and place a bucket of water, which will create a 1 x 1 block of water. You can jump and land into any depth of water from any height and not receive any damage at all.

Crafting:

- 6 Stone Blocks / Wood Planks = 4 Stairs
- 7 Sticks = 3 Ladders

Step 8: Branch Mining

Once you have dug your shaft mine, you can start to go out and do branch mining. This is good when you have gotten to a level that should have the resources you want. It will give you more chances of running into that resource. In order to be the most efficient with this method, you are going to want to dig out one-block branches, leaving three blocks in between them. This will result in the most space being covered and the greatest likelihood that resources will not be missed.

Step 9: Quarry Mining

Quarry mining covers the most space while mining. When creating a quarry you need to decide 1) how big of a quarry you want and 2) how you are going to get back out. Start by digging out your first layer of the quarry. You may want to consider starting no higher than sea level, as some of the ores can't be found until you've gone down a ways. Take into consideration how you are going to get in and out of this quarry, i.e., if you need a ladder, decide where it is going to be located and start placing it; if you are going to create a staircase, get it started. Then you just keep digging down!

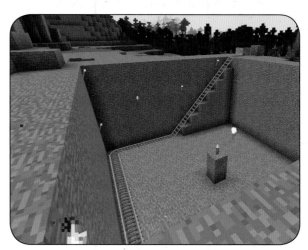

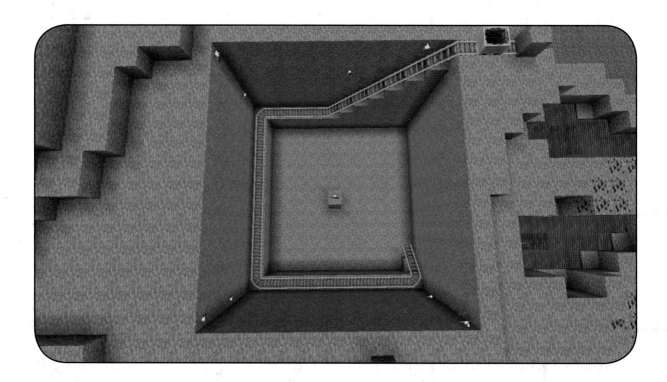

How to Farm

Nicole Smith

http://www.instructables.com/id/Farming-in-Minecraft/

Farming can be almost as important as mining in Minecraft. Farming will give you food to eat and will also provide you with supplies you cannot get otherwise. There is basic vegetable and melon farming, but you can also farm trees, mushrooms, cacti, sugar cane, and cocoa beans.

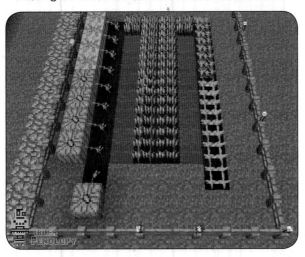

Step 1: Farm Setup and Tools

Time to get started farming! There are some tools that are nice to have before you get started.

Tools

- Hoe—two sticks stacked in the middle and then two of the material you want to make it out of on top and also in the top right square = a hoe
- Fence - six sticks in two rows next to each other = two fences
- Fence gate - four sticks on either side of two wooden planks = one gate
- Torches are good since most plants need light to grow. One stick below one piece of coal = four torches
- Water - plants need water to grow, but most plants do not need to be planted directly next to water to grow. You need at least one block of water for a 9 x 9 section of land (the water would be in the middle). You can use iron buckets to gather water or you can farm next to existing water.
- Bone meal - created from bones (which can be obtained when you kill skeletons) and used to accelerate the growth of plants.

Farm Setup

- Clear some land. It is nice to have land that is not near a hill, since animals can jump down from a hill into your fenced off land.

- You will use your hoe to create farmland. Using it will make the soil appear to have rows on it.
- Fences are nice to keep mobs out of your farms. Sometimes plants can be destroyed by trampling, and who wants a creeper destroying all their hard work? Why use a fence instead of just blocks? Anything can jump on top of one block, but a fence is 1.5 blocks high, so only spiders can jump over them (or anyone standing on a plateau or hill nearby).
- You can just break a piece of fence to get in or you can create a gate, which is handier.
- When you pour water in a long hole (as I have shown) it will flow unless you continue to pour water in at different spots. The holes you see I have created each needed five buckets of water to make the water stop flowing.
- Torches can very handily sit on top of the fence posts.

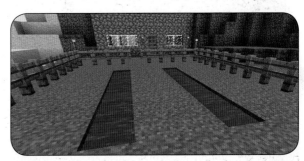

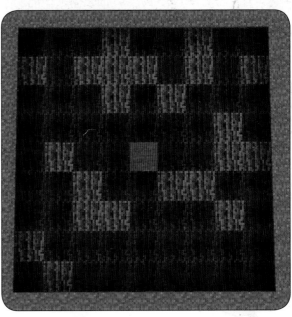

Step 2: Wheat
Planting
- Wheat needs to be planted on farmland and needs water, but it does not need to be right next to water to grow. However, if it is planted next to water, the farmland will be hydrated and it will help the plant grow faster.
- You can collect seeds by destroying grass. Not all grass will produce seeds, but if you just start destroying a field of grass, you will end up with quite a few.
- The tips of the soil will turn brown and the rest of it will turn more yellow when it is ready to harvest.
- When you harvest wheat, you will get wheat and then one or more seeds to plant more.

Facts about Wheat
- Wheat is used to make hay bales (for decoration) and wheat (to eat). It cannot be eaten as is.
- Wheat is used for making cakes and cookies.
- Wheat is probably the most commonly farmed plant in Minecraft. It is really easy to obtain seeds and grow some.
- Wheat is used for breeding animals, including sheep and cows.
- The seeds used to grow wheat are used to breed chickens.
- It is found in about every village garden.

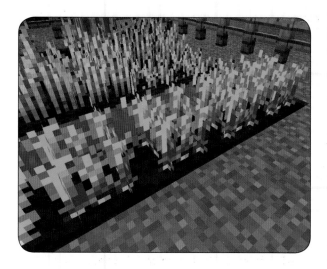

Step 3: Carrots and Potatoes
Planting Carrots
- Carrots grow on farmland block.
- Unlike wheat, you plant a carrot to grow carrots (instead of planting seeds).
- The tops of the carrots will show when ready to be harvested.

Facts about Carrots
- Can be eaten raw and cannot be cooked.
- Used to breed pigs.
- Can be attached to a fishing pole and can be used to ride pigs in combination with saddles.
- Can be found in village gardens.
- Sometimes dropped by zombies when killed, but this is rare.

Planting Potatoes
- Grows on farmland block.
- Planted directly in soil like carrots (no seeds).
- Will start to show when it is ready to be harvested.

Facts about Potatoes
- Can be found in village gardens.
- Once in a while a zombie will drop one when killed, but it is rare.
- Can be eaten raw but has only one food point.
- Can be cooked in a furnace to make a baked potato.
- Can result in a poisonous potato when harvested (a very small possibility).

Step 4: Pumpkins and Melons
Planting Pumpkins
- When you break a pumpkin, you get a full pumpkin. In order to plant more, you need to use the crafting table to get seeds.
- Needs to be planted on farmland, but does not need a farmland block for the pumpkin to appear on.
- Unlike the previous plants mentioned, you plant the pumpkin and that is where the stem will grow; the pumpkin will appear in an adjacent square, so you always need a space available next to it.
- When you collect a pumpkin, the block below it will turn to dirt even if it had been plowed to be farmland.
- After you harvest the pumpkin the stalk stays, so you don't have to replant it over and over again. It will continue to grow from that stalk. If you do break the stalk, you will get pumpkin seeds.

Facts about Pumpkins
- They can be rare, but appear in many biomes.
- Pumpkins always have a face. The direction of the face depends on where you are facing when you place it.
- They can be made into a Jack o' Lantern by using the crafting table. Stack one pumpkin on top of one torch for one Jack o' Lantern.

- Can be worn as helmet, but provides no protection and impairs your vision if doing first person perspective.
- Pumpkins can be used to make Snow Golems and Iron Golems—the pumpkin has to be placed last.
- Will emit light under water.

Planting Melons
- Found in the jungle, but you can also find them in chests in mines and get them by trading with villagers.
- When you find a melon, break it to get melon pieces and then craft the melon pieces into seeds.
- Just like the pumpkin, you plant the seed on a farmland block and this will create a stalk which will produce a melon on an adjacent square.
- Just like the pumpkin, the stalk will stay after you harvest the melon and you can destroy the stalk to get seeds.

Facts about Melons
- Each melon block should drop 3–7 melon slices.
- Eating a melon doesn't provide much nourishment.
- If you want a melon block it takes nine melon pieces but once you break that block you have created you will only get the 3–7 slices, as mentioned. It's not really worth making unless you want it for decorative purposes.

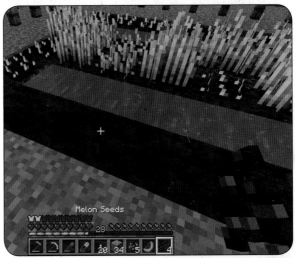

Step 5: Cactus and Sugar Cane
Cactus
- Find them on sand in the desert.
- They will hurt if you touch them.
- Can destroy anything, including mobs and items.
- Used for garbage disposal since they can destroy items.
- Cook in furnace to make green dye.

- The easiest way to harvest it is by destroying the block below it or destroying the bottom block of the cactus.
- Just place it to start growing it.

Sugar Cane
- Can grow on dirt, sand, or grass in any biome with water.
- Can only be planted/grow next to water—will not grow by ice.
- Most commonly grows three blocks high.
- Will continue to grow if you break all but the bottom.
- Can be stacked as high as you want.
- Can be used to make sugar (one in a recipe for cake and pumpkin pie) or paper (three in a row) for books, bookshelves, and maps.
- Does not need farmland block to grow
- Can be planted underwater and creates air pockets that you can breathe in.

Step 6: Mushroom Farming
- When mushroom farming, you can't have a light level greater than 12 or they won't grow. Torches give off 14, so you don't want direct light on your mushrooms. Light does not matter if they are grown on a mycelium or podzol block.
- They do not require water to grow.
- Using bone meal on either a red or brown mushroom will cause a huge mushroom.
- You can use a shovel on a huge mushroom to collect mushrooms.
- For planting them, I dug stairs down and made sure light from the outside didn't spill in (though some light can get in). I dug about four squares up in the ceiling and placed a torch. I did this two times. I made the room only two blocks high with a dirt floor (you can't place mushrooms on stone, though I have seen them in the wild on stone). Now wait. It takes quite a while for the mushrooms to spread.

Step 7: Cocoa Beans
- Cocoa beans aren't very useful, but if you want cookies or brown dye, you will need them. They also just look fun and can be used for decorating.
- They can be found in the jungle.
- Cocoa pods can only be grown on jungle wood, but the wood doesn't have to be a tree (you can just stack blocks of jungle wood).

- Beans can just be placed on a tree for planting.
- Their growing process has them go from green to yellowish to reddish orange.

Step 8: Trees

Time to plant trees! Why plant trees? It's nice to be able to control your wood supply and to control the type of wood you have access to.

Common Characteristics of all 6 Types of Trees

- You can punch wood to harvest it, or you can use an ax.
- You can punch the leaves as well, and they are very easy to destroy, but you can also use shears to more quickly destroy leaves.
- You will find that wood is one of the most essential materials in the game.
- When you destroy all the wood of a tree, the leaves will slowly disappear and drop anything they may be holding (seeds or apples in some instances).
- You will always get a block of wood when destroying wood, but you won't always get something from a block of leaves.
- You should try to clear an area to plant your trees so that they have room to grow.

Oak

- Has medium-colored wood.
- Grows tall.
- Is very common.
- Has a chance of giving you apples from the leaves.

Dark Oak

- Has darkest color of wood.
- Is harder to find than regular oak.
- Cannot just grow from one sapling planted; requires four saplings (2 x 2) to grow.
- Has a chance of giving you apples from leaves.

Spruce

- Has dark-colored wood.
- Grows tall.
- Can be planted with four saplings (2 x 2) to get a bigger tree.

Birch

- Has lightest color of wood.

- Grows quickly.
- Doesn't grow very tall, easy to harvest all.

Acacia

- Has a unique red color only found in the savanna.
- Instead of growing straight up, as is normal for Minecraft trees, it grows in a strange growth formation (can grow diagonally with blocks not necessarily right next to each other).

Jungle

- Has medium-colored wood.
- Grows to an enormous size (makes it very difficult to harvest the whole tree). I have also seen them grow very small like bushes (those cover the ground in the jungle).
- Only found in jungles.
- Can grow cocoa beans on them.
- Can be grown with four saplings (2 x 2); vines can grow on them, and you can climb them.

Step 9: Bonus: Garden Shed

I have been playing my survival game for a while and I have accumulated so much stuff. I have about five double chests with various supplies separated into them. After gathering some acacia wood, I decided to make a shed (because I like the red wood). In my shed I kept seeds (not including things that can be eaten, such as pumpkins and melons), plants, natural materials (snowballs, lily pads, and grass), and tools used for farming and animals, including hoes, shears, and axes. The interior dimensions were 4 x 3 (so the blocks were placed in a 6 x 5 rectangle to create the walls. The basic height is 3 blocks high, not including the half spaces that were left from the slab roof.

Supplies I Used
- Acacia planks (walls and table)
- Acacia wood slabs (roof and overhang)
- Birch planks (floor)
- Wooden door
- Glass panes
- Double chest
- Crafting block
- Clay (smelted and then made into a pot)
- Flowers (decoration)
- Cobblestone (path to front door of home)

Mining Ores
Nicole Smith
http://www.instructables.com/id/
Mining-in-Minecraft/

Minecraft wouldn't be what it is without mining! In this Instructable I will go over all the different ores and special resources you can mine in the game as well as the awesome things you can do with them!

	Coal	Iron	Gold	Lapis Lazuli	Diamond	Redstone	Obsidian	Emerald
Ore	■	■	■	■	■	■	■	■
Drops	●			●	◆	●		◇
Smelt		▭	▭					
Block	■	◻	◻	◼	◻	◼		◻

Step 1: Furnace and Smelting

In order to craft some items, you will need to smelt an ore into an ingot. To smelt you need to build a furnace out of 8 cobblestones. To smelt with the furnace, first place it like you would on a crafting table. To use, put the ore you want to smelt in the top spot and a fuel in the bottom spot (fuels can include coal, charcoal, wood, and a bucket of lava). The ingot you create will show up on the right.

Step 2: Coal
Facts about Coal
- Is most common ore.
- Must be mined with a pickax, but it can be mined with just a wooden one.
- Used for fuel in furnace.
- Results in a piece of coal when a block of it is destroyed.
- Can be found at any level in the world as long as there is stone for it to form next to.

Crafting with Coal
- 9 Coal = 1 Coal Block and vice versa
- 1 Coal + 1 Stick = 4 Torches
- 1 Coal + 1 Gunpowder + Blaze = Fire Charge

Step 3: Iron
Facts about Iron
- Mined by using a stone pickax or better.
- When destroyed will drop the iron ore block.
- Will appear in levels 63 (one block above sea level) and lower.
- Used, as with any material, to make iron tools and weapons.
- Used, as with any material, to make iron armor.
- When smelted yields iron ingots.

Crafting with Iron
- 9 Iron Ingots = 1 Block of Iron and vice versa
- 3 Iron Ingots in a "V" shape = Iron Bucket
- 2 Iron Ingots diagonal from each other = Shears
- 1 Iron Ingot + 1 Flint = Flint and Steel (for starting fires)
- 5 Iron Ingots in a "U" shape = Minecart
- 6 Iron Ingots + 1 Stick = 16 Rails
- 6 Iron Ingots + 1 Redstone Torch in the center + 2 Sticks above and below the torch = 6 Activator Rails
- 6 Iron Ingots + 1 Redstone + 1 Stone Pressure Plate = 6 Detector Rails
- 7 Iron Ingots in a big "U" shape = Cauldron
- 4 Iron Ingots + 1 Redstone = Compass
- 3 Iron Blocks + 4 Iron Ingots below = Anvil
- 5 Iron Ingots + Chest = Hopper
- 6 Iron Ingots (in two columns) = 1 Iron Door
- 6 Iron Ingots (in two rows) = 16 Iron Bars
- 2 Iron Ingots = Weighted Pressure Plate
- 1 Iron Ingot + 6 Wooden Planks + 4 Cobblestone + 1 Redstone = Piston

- 1 Iron Ingot + 1 Stick + 1 Wooden Plank = Tripwire Hook
- 6 Iron Ingots (in two rows, top and bottom) + 3 Diamonds = Nether Core Reactor

Step 4: Gold
Facts about Gold
- Mined with iron pickax or better.
- When mined, will drop one gold ore block.
- Appears in bottom 32 layers of the world.
- Used, as with any material, to make golden tools and weapons.
- Used, as with any material, to make golden armor.
- Is very strong when used to make tools (can mine it quickly), but is not very durable (will break quicker).
- When smelted, results in gold ingots.

Crafting with Gold
- Craft 1 Gold Ingot = 9 Gold Nuggets and vice versa
- Craft 9 Gold Ingots = 1 Gold Block and vice versa
- Craft 4 Iron Ingots (in each edge middle) + Redstone in the center = Clock
- 8 Gold Ingots surrounding 1 Apple = 1 Golden Apple
- 8 Gold Blocks surrounding 1 Apple = Enchanted Golden Apple
- 8 Gold Nuggets surrounding 1 Carrot = 1 Gold Carrot
- 8 Gold Nuggets surrounding 1 Melon Slice = Glistening Melon

Step 5: Lapis Lazuli
Facts about Lapis Lazuli
- Mined with an iron pickax or better.
- Will drop four or more pieces when its ore is mined.
- Found in layers 31 and lower in the game.
- Is a primary dye.
- Applied to sheep to dye them.

- Applied to tamed wolves to dye their collars.
- Can be used to dye leather armor.

Crafting with Lapis Lazuli
- 9 Pieces = 1 Lapis Lazuli Block and vice versa
- 1 Lapis Lazuli + 1 Wool = 1 Blue Wool
- 8 blocks of Hardened Clay + 1 Lapis Lazuli = 8 Blue-Stained Clay
- 8 Glass Blocks + 1 Lapis Lazuli = 9 Blue-Stained Glass

Dye Combinations (when you mix dye with another dye you will get an outcome with an equal amount of dye):
- 1 Lapis Lazuli + 1 Green Dye = 2 Cyan Dye
- 1 Lapis Lazuli + 1 Bone Meal = 2 Light Blue Dye
- 1 Lapis Lazuli + 1 Bone Meal + 2 Red Rose = 4 Magenta Dye
- 1 Lapis Lazuli + 1 Pink Dye + 1 Rose Red = 3 Magenta Dye
- 1 Lapis Lazuli + 1 Rose Red = 2 Purple Dye

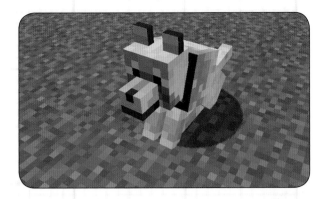

Step 6: Diamond
Facts about Diamonds
- Mined by using an iron pickax or better.
- Drops a diamond gem when mined.
- Found in layers 15 and lower in the world.
- Use it, as with any material, to make diamond tools and weapons.
- Use it, as with any material, to make diamond armor.

Crafting with Diamonds
- Craft 9 Gems = 1 Diamond Block and vice versa
- Craft 8 Wood Plans surrounding 1 Diamond Gem = Jukebox
- Craft 1 Book + 2 Diamond Gems + 4 Blocks of Obsidian = Enchantment Table
- Craft 3 Diamond Gems + 6 Iron Ingots = Nether Reactor Core (in Pocket Edition [PE] only)

Step 7: Redstone
Facts about Redstone
- Mined by using an iron pickax or better.
- Results in multiple Redstone blocks when ore is mined.
- Found in layers 16 and lower in the world.
- Used as a potion ingredient in brewing.
- When it is placed it becomes redstone dust and is used to create circuits.

- Redstone dust will be dark in color when it has no power running through it, and will turn bright red when powered.

Crafting with Redstone
- 9 Redstone = 1 Redstone Box and vice versa
- 1 Redstone + 1 Stick = Redstone Torch
- 1 Redstone + 4 Iron Ingots = Compass
- 1 Redstone + 4 Gold Ingots = Clock
- 1 Redstone + 1 Stone Pressure Plate + 6 Iron Ingots = Detector Rail
- 1 Redstone + 6 Gold Ingots + 1 Stick = Powered Rail
- 1 Redstone + 3 Stones + 2 Redstone Torches = Redstone Repeater
- 1 Redstone + 7 Cobblestones + 1 Bow = Dispenser
- 1 Redstone + 7 Cobblestones = Dropper
- 1 Redstone + 8 Wooden Planks around it = Note Block
- 1 Redstone + 4 Cobblestones + 1 Iron Ingot + 3 Wood Planks = Piston
- 4 Redstone + 1 Glowstone = Redstone Lamp

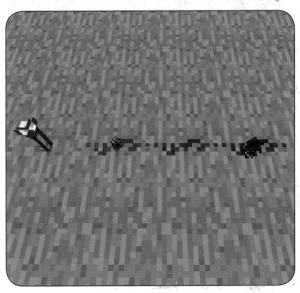

Step 8: Obsidian

Facts about Obsidian

- Can only be mined by a diamond pickax.
- Is the second-toughest block in the game next to bedrock.
- Is immune to almost all explosions.
- Instead of just forming in the game, it is formed by the environment in the game—it is created when flowing water hits a lava source block.
- Is not formed from lava hitting water—that creates cobblestone.
- Created by water flowing into lava, and even if you are able to clear the lava from on top, there will probably be some underneath making it difficult to mine. If you mine the obsidian and there is lava underneath, it will destroy the piece of obsidian you just mined.
- Used to create a Nether Portal to go to the Nether— made by making a standing 4 x 5 obsidian rectangle and then igniting the center with flint and steel (this will create a see-through purple haze).
- Can't be moved by pistons.

Crafting with Obsidian

- 4 Obsidian Blocks + 1 Book + 2 Diamonds = Enchantment Table
- 3 Obsidian Blocks + 5 Blocks of Glass + Nether Star = Beacon
- 8 Obsidian Blocks + Eye of Ender = Ender Chest (acts like a normal chest for storage, except you can access contents of one Ender Chest from another)

Mining Obsidian

- You will, undoubtedly, develop your own technique for mining obsidian, but I wanted to share one way I have tackled it. (I've put notes on the pictures to help.) Block off water and lava flows (keeps you safe); you can even completely stop flows if you find where the source is and block it off with a block of stone.
- Find the edge of the obsidian and dig down. Your goal is to work your way around the obsidian "lake" and put cobblestone below the obsidian blocks before mining them.
- Once you get around the edge of the obsidian, try to dig down so you can get to the blocks below the obsidian.
- Once you are there, destroy the block on the edge that reveals the lava under the obsidian. Place cobblestone under the obsidian block you want to mine.
- Go ahead and mine that obsidian.
- Repeat (this takes a long time, but you guarantee you won't destroy the blocks in the lava this way).

Step 9: Create Your Own Obsidian

If you don't want to venture underground look-ing for places obsidian has formed, you can create your own!

- First, you have to find a lava lake (not a lava fall, as that won't help you here—it needs to be standing lava). Go to one edge and create a little indent; it only needs to be one block (I did three blocks). You don't *have* to create an indent, but if you do, you can control the flow of the lava, as if you just drop it near the edge it will go everywhere. Drop your bucket of water so it flows into the lava.
- Once it has spread out as far as it is going to go, either pick the water source back up or block it off so it stops flowing.
- You have created a obsidian block.
- You will still probably have lava below it, so take your time and carefully mine it all out.

Step 10: Emerald

Facts about Emeralds

- Used as a currency in the game; you can usually trade with villagers for them.
- Can only be naturally found in extreme hill biomes, unlike other ores.
- Shows up between levels 4 and 32 of the world.
- Mined using an iron or diamond pickax.
- Drops one emerald per ore.
- Cannot be used to make tools or armor.

Crafting with Emeralds

These can only be crafted to make an emerald block and vice versa.

Step 11: Tools and Armor

Out of all the ores, you can only make weapons, tools, and armor out of iron, gold, and diamonds. They all have different durability and strength, and are crafted in the same way for each ore.

Crafting Ore Tools (stone, iron, diamond, and gold shown; can also be made from cobblestone and wooden planks)

- 1 Ore + 2 Sticks = Shovel
- 3 Ores + 2 Sticks = Ax
- 3 Ores + 2 Sticks = Pickax
- 2 Ores + 1 Stick = Sword
- 2 Ores + 2 Sticks = Hoe

Crafting Armor (iron, diamond, and gold shown; can also be crafted from leather and can be found made of chain)

- 5 Ores (in an upside down "U" shape) = Helmet
- 8 Ores (in all spots but top middle) = Chestplate
- 7 Ores (in large upside down "U" shape)
  = Leggings
- 4 Ores (in two little columns) = Boots

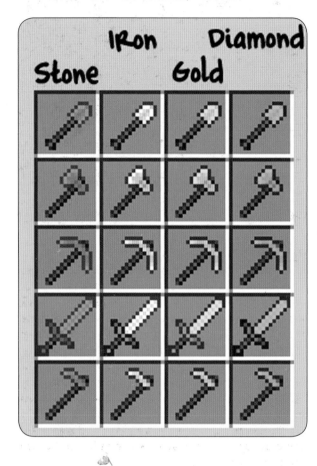

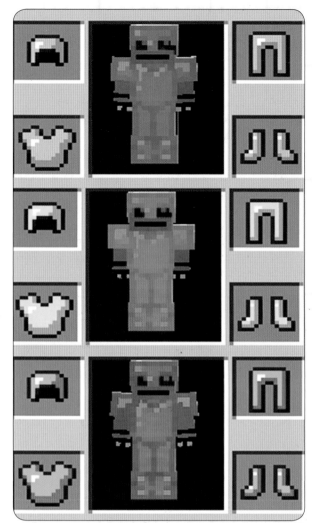

How to Fight Monsters

Nicole Smith

http://www.instructables.com/id/Fighting-Monsters-in-Minecraft/

In order to fight your enemy, you must know your enemy! You could just choose to avoid all of the hostile mobs in Minecraft, but you can get things from them that are either hard or impossible to get elsewhere. So, before you venture out at night or into the dark depths of the caves, read up on your enemy and be ready to fight!

Step 1: Weapons and Armor

If you are going to fight monsters, you need to be properly prepared.

Crafting Weapons
- 1 Stick + 2 (Wood Planks | Gold Ingots | Cobblestone| Iron Ingots | Diamond) = 1 Sword
- 3 Sticks + 3 Pieces of String = 1 Bow
- 1 Stick + 1 Feather + 1 Piece of Flint = 4 Arrows

Armor
- 5 Ores (in an upside down "U") = Helmet
- 8 Ores (in all spots but top middle) = Chestplate
- 7 Ores (in large upside down "U") = Leggings
- 4 Ores (in two little columns) = Boots

Step 2: Creepers

Facts about Creepers
- Does not spawn in the light like other hostile mobs, but can survive in daylight.
- Is frightened off by cats and ocelots.
- Fights by exploding when within close proximity to the player.
- Will drop gunpowder if it is killed (will not drop if it explodes).

- Will drop music discs if it is killed by a skeleton.
- Cannot walk over a rail on flat ground.

Fighting a Creeper

The best way to approach fighting a creeper is to hit it and back away. If you don't back up far enough, fast enough, it will explode. If you back away far enough and fast enough, it will not explode and will head towards you again, giving you another opportunity to hit and kill it.

A safer way of engaging a creeper is with a bow and arrow. Since you can only trigger a creeper by being close to it, it won't blow up when shot with an arrow.

If a creeper is in an area in which you do not want it to blow up, lead it away to water, as it won't cause damage in open water.

Step 3: Zombie, Zombie Villagers, and Chicken Jockey

Facts about Zombies
- Will spawn in the dark and, unlike a creeper, will light on fire in daylight.
- Is most common hostile mob in the game.
- Fights by hitting you.
- Has variations including a zombie villager and baby zombie.
- Can spawn using weapons and wearing armor.
- Zombie villagers can be cured with a potion.
- When killed, can drop the following: rotten flesh (most likely), carrots, potatoes, and iron ingots (all rarely).
- Can pick up items you drop.

Facts about Baby Zombies
- Will create a chicken jockey if it rides a chicken.
- Runs faster than normal zombies.
- Won't burn in sunlight like normal zombies.
- Can fit through 1 x 1 gaps.

Fighting a Zombie

These can be fought with any weapon. If attacking with a sword, you can stand one block above it and this will make it less likely that the zombie will be able to hit you, as long as you continuously attack it until it is killed.

Step 4: Spiders and Cave Spiders

Facts about Spiders

- Are a neutral mob when in higher light levels and are hostile when in a lower light level; if you run into them at night, they will attack you, and if you attack a neutral spider in daylight, it will defend itself and attack back.
- Look the same, except the cave spider is blue and smaller than a normal spider.
- Do not burn up in sunlight.
- Cave spiders are poisonous: the poison cannot kill you itself, it will only bring you down to one heart at most.
- Can climb up blocks vertically.
- While spiders spawn naturally in the game, cave spiders only come from monster spawners from mine shafts.
- Can both drop string and spider eyes when killed.
- Can form with a skeleton on its back, making a spider jockey.
- Can jump two or three blocks, making them able to jump over fences that are 1.5 blocks tall.
- Cave spiders are smaller than normal spiders and are less than a block in width, length, and height.

Fighting Spiders

Like many of the monsters, it is easiest to attack them from a distance. Fighting normal spiders face to face can be difficult since they jump around a lot, but because they are 2 blocks wide by 2 blocks long, you can dig a trench that is only 1 block wide and attack them from below and they won't be able to go down into the trench.

Step 5: Skeleton and Spider Jockey

Facts about Skeletons

- Will spawn in the dark and will light on fire in daylight.
- Is one of the most common hostile mobs in the game.
- Fights by shooting you with arrows.
- When killed, can drop the following: arrows and bones (most likely); bow (least likely).
- Can be evaded by hiding inside sugar cane.
- Can have their arrows avoided by you hiding behind things.
- Can wear head armor, which will protect them from burning in sunlight.
- Cannot see you through vines.
- Can have their arrows blocked by a sword.

Facts about Spider Jockeys

- Is a skeleton riding a spider.
- Rarely appears.
- Both the spider and skeleton attack in their usual way (making them twice as deadly) and will each need to be killed.
- When killed, can drop the following: arrows, bones, string, and spider eye (most likely); bow (rarely).

Fighting a Skeleton and Spider Jockey:

The best and safest way to fight a skeleton is with a bow and arrow. When they get close enough to you, they stop walking and start shooting, so when you try to run up to them to just hit them, they will continuously hit you with arrows.

If you are going for a melee option, try to sneak up on them, coming at them from the site or above so you can hit them.

Another option is to trick the skeleton into shooting another hostile mob, and then that mob will attack the skeleton and they will fight each other.

Lure them underwater and attack them from below; they won't/can't sink down to attack you.

Step 6: Slime
Facts about Slime

- Appears as a green cube and, when attacked, will break into smaller cubes.
- When small slimes are killed, can drop slimeballs.
- Usually spawns in layer 40 or lower, or in swamps (when spawning in a swamp, it will most likely need to be a full moon); can possibly spawn in any light level.
- Has three sizes: large, medium, and small; you can run into any size slime and only the smallest slime will drop anything when killed.
- Jumps around to move.

Fighting Slime

Use melee attack to attack slime. It will break into smaller pieces. When those pieces are attacked, they turn into even smaller pieces. When you destroy those pieces, they die and do not continue to split up.

Step 7: Witches
Facts about Witches

- Spawn in witch's huts, which can be found in swamps.
- Do not burn in sunlight.
- Look like villagers except for outfit, a wart on their nose, and a witch's hat.

- When killed, can drop the following: glass bottle, spider eye, sugar, glowstone dust, gunpowder, redstone, or stick (most likely); potions of healing, fire resistance, swiftness, and water breathing (rarely, when killed while drinking a potion).
- Attacks with potions.

Note: Milk can be used to nullify effects from potions they use on you

Fighting Witches

The best way to attack witches is with a bow from a distance out of range of their potions. If you don't have a bow, sprint at her and attack before she can do anything.

Step 8: Silverfish
Facts about Silverfish

- Spawn when a monster egg is destroyed, which will look like an ordinary stone block.
- When you attack them, other nearby silverfish could be called to attack.
- If you leave it alone, it will crawl into another block, making it a monster egg.
- Does not drop anything when killed.

Fighting Silverfish

Since the silverfish is small and cannot climb or jump, it is safest to attack from atop a two-block pole. Attacking it will draw other nearby silverfish from monster eggs unless it is killed in one hit.

Step 9: Endermen

Facts about Endermen
- Are found in the Overworld and The End.
- Are neutral but will attack you if you attack them or look at them; you can look at them out of the corner of the screen but do not look at their face.
- They will pick up/steal blocks they find.
- Can teleport.
- Can drop ender pearl when killed.
- Take damage from water and rain.
- Can be looked at through glass, while you are wearing a pumpkin on your head, or when you are in a boat or minecart, without provoking them.

Fighting Endermen

Since you can't provoke them just by looking at them if you wear a pumpkin, it is wise to wear one when going to attack. Since they are tall, you can go into an area that is only two blocks high and attempt to attack from there.

Since water is dangerous to them, fight them when they are near water and try to hit them in it. You can also stand in water and provoke them. They won't attack right away but they will eventually follow you into the water and take the damage. After attacking, they will teleport away, so try to kill them before they can do that.

Falling from a cliff can kill them since they cannot teleport while they are falling.

Nether Mobs

The following mobs are only found in the Nether and are difficult to kill.

Beware!

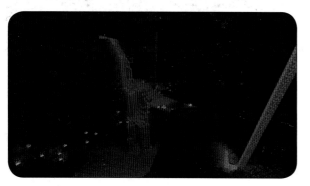

Step 10: Blaze

Facts about Blaze
- Found in the Nether.
- Can fly and shoot fire charges.
- Is not damaged by fire or lava.
- Besides being hurt by normal weapons, can be attacked with snowballs.
- When killed, can drop the following: blaze rods and glowstone dust.
- A very difficult mob to fight—attacks are unblockable and come fast.

Fighting a Blaze

Snowballs are a great method of attack as they do pretty decent damage, and you can throw them from a distance.

You can use wolves to fight blaze, but they can be set on fire and killed.

Step 11: Ghast

Facts about Ghast
- Found in the Nether.
- Resistant to water and lava.
- When killed, can drop the following: gunpowder and ghast tear.
- Does not go after a player, instead attacks from afar.
- Will open its mouth and eyes when attacking.
- You can deflect fireballs with arrow or melee attack (no weapon needed).

Fighting Ghasts
- Easiest to attack and kill with a bow and arrow.
- Deflect fireballs back at them to hurt and kill them.
- Can be attacked and killed with melee weapons, and you can lure them closer with a fishing rod.

- Are not burned by fire or lava.
- Can pick up items and use them.
- When killed, can drop coal and bone.
- When attacked, will inflict the wither effect on you.
- Attacks fast.
- If it gets a bow, it will shoot fire arrows at you.

Fighting Wither Skeletons

The best way to attack is with a melee attack. Hit them and jump back out of the way. Repeat until you have killed them. Can be shot with a bow, but they are fast and harder to hit than other mobs.

Step 14: Monster Spawner

A monster spawner is a one-block-sized cage that will spawn monsters. They will appear to have fire and mini monsters inside of them. They can be destroyed with weapons, including pickax, sword, and ax.

Monster Spawners can be commonly found in dungeons, which will be identified by moss, stones, and chests. They are also found in abandoned mine shafts.

Step 12: Magma Cube

Facts about Magma Cube

- Found in the Nether.
- Appears as a cube and, when confronted, separates into eight layers.
- When killed can drop magma cream.
- When killed will release two to four smaller versions of itself.
- Is not burned by fire or lava.

Fighting Magma Cubes

The large magma cube is difficult to kill with just a sword; it is best to use a bow from a distance. Once it is broken up into smaller cubes you can more easily kill them with melee attacks.

Step 13: Wither Skeleton

Facts about Wither Skeleton

- Spawn in the Nether in nether fortresses.
- Are considered the Nether equivalent of a skeleton; they look the same but are dark gray instead of light gray.
- Attack you with stone swords.

Animals

Nicole Smith

http://www.instructables.com/id/Minecraft-Animals/

The animals in Minecraft are referred to as passive mobs. All living creatures in Minecraft are called mobs, and they are either passive, neutral, or hostile. In this Instructable I'm going to talk about the passive and the neutral mobs that don't usually cause you harm.

Step 1: Leading Animals

You can use leads with passive mobs. Just use it like you would anything else while pointing at the animal. You can tow them around behind you or you can attach the lead to a fence post to make the animal stay in place.

Crafting:

- 4 Strings + 1 Slimeball = 2 Leads

Step 2: Sheep

Facts about Sheep

- Sheep provide you with wool, which can be obtained by killing the sheep or shearing it with shears (if you kill a sheep you will always get only one block of wool, whereas if you shear it you have the opportunity to get up to three).
- Killing a baby sheep gets you nothing.
- A sheep can be dyed itself, or you can dye the wool you get from the sheep; once a sheep is dyed it will always be that color no matter how many times it has been shorn, but it can be re-dyed.
- Breed a sheep using wheat.
- When breeding sheep of different colors together you will either get one color or the other, or you will get a whole new color if the colors are compatible to making a new one.
- Wool is needed to make beds.

Crafting

- 3 Wood Planks + 3 Wool Blocks = 1 Bed

Crafting Dye

- Poppy / Rose Bush / Red Tulip = Rose Red
- Orange Tulip = Orange
- Dandelion / Sunflower = Dandelion Yellow
- Blue Orchid = Light Blue
- Lilac / Allium = Magenta
- Peony / Pink Tulips = Pink
- Azure Blue / Oxeye Daisy / White Tulip = Light Gray

Dye Combinations

- Lapis Lazuli + Cactus Green = Cyan
- Lapis Lazuli + Bone Meal = Light Blue
- Lapis Lazuli + Bone Meal + 2 Rose Red = Magenta
- Lapis Lazuli + Pink + Rose Red = Magenta
- Rose Red + Lapis Lazuli = Purple
- Rose Red + Bone Meal = Light Pink
- Orange + Dandelion Yellow = Orange
- Ink Sac from Squid + Bone Meal = Gray
- Cactus Green + Bone Meal = Lime Green
- Gray + Bone Meal = Light Gray
- Purple + Pink = Magenta

Other Dyes

- Cook Cactus in Furnace = Cactus Green
- Ink Sac from Squid = Black
- Bone Meal crafted from Bone = White
- Cocoa Beans = Brown
- Lapis Lazuli = Blue

Step 3: Pigs

Facts about Pigs

- Pigs drop a raw pork chop when killed (if killed by fire or lava you can get a cooked pork chop if the pork chop isn't destroyed by the fire first).
- Pigs can be saddled, but a saddle cannot be taken back off of it.
- Breed pigs with carrots.
- If a pig is struck by lightning, it will turn into a zombie pigman.

Riding Pigs

- A pig can be ridden when you put a saddle on it.
- In order to ride it, get on the saddled pig and lead it around with a carrot on a stick.
- The carrot will eventually be eaten by the pig.

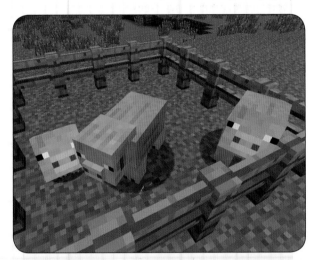

Step 4: Cows and Mooshrooms

Facts about Cows

- Cows drop raw beef and leather when killed.
- Cows can be milked over and over again with an iron bucket to get milk; milk can be consumed as an antidote for poison or used as an ingredient in cooking.
- Breed cows using wheat.
- Baby cows will not drop anything when killed, but can provide milk.

Facts about Mooshrooms

- Only found in the Mooshroom Biome.
- Look like a cow except for color and the mushrooms growing on its back.

- Mooshrooms drop raw beef and leather when killed.
- Can be milked over and over again with an iron bucket to get milk.
- Can be milked over and over again with a wooden bowl to get mushroom soup.
- Breed using wheat.
- Shear a mooshroom with shears to get red mushrooms (once sheared it will turn into a normal cow and cannot change back).
- Baby mooshrooms will not drop anything when killed, but can provide milk and be sheared for mushrooms.

Step 5: Chickens

Facts about Chickens

- Chickens can drop raw chicken and feathers when killed.
- Chickens lay eggs, which can be used for recipes, or you can throw and break them with a chance you will get a baby chick.
- Breed them using wheat, melon, or pumpkin seeds.
- Unlike other animals, when they fall off a cliff, they won't take damage or die because they will flap their wings, which slows their descent.

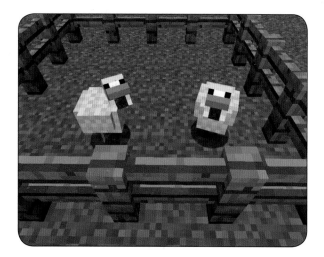

Step 6: Horses, Donkeys, and Mules

Facts about Horses

- Horses only spawn in the plains or savannah.
- Do not spawn very commonly.
- Drop leather when killed.
- Once a horse is tamed, you can breed it, equip with saddle and armor (both a saddle and horse armor cannot be made, they must be found), and ride it.
- To ride on it and control it, the horse must be equipped with a saddle.
- Breed using a golden carrot or a golden apple.
- Unlike other tamed animals, a horse will not follow you once tamed.
- Babies of tamed horses will still need to be tamed when grown.
- Baby horses can be fed golden apples, golden carrots, apples, wheat, hay bale, bread, and sugar to speed up growing.
- Jumping while riding a saddled horse causes the horse to jump.
- While riding a horse you can jump over fences and stone walls.

Facts about Donkeys

- Only spawn in the plains and savannah.
- Spawn less often then horses.
- Drops leather when killed.
- Breed with golden carrot or golden apple.
- Needs to be tamed to equip it with anything; you repeatedly try to ride it until you get hearts to tame.
- Cannot be equipped with armor, but can be equipped with a saddle and chest once tamed (provides 15 inventory slots; chest cannot be removed once equipped unless the animal dies, then it will be dropped).
- There are no variations in donkeys, they all look the same.

Facts about Mules

- Created by breeding a horse with a donkey; does not appear naturally in the game.

- Cannot breed.
- Drops leather when killed.
- Cannot be equipped with armor, but can be equipped with a saddle and chest once tamed (provides 15 inventory slots; chest cannot be removed once equipped unless the animal dies, then it will be dropped).
- All mules look the same.

Taming Horses, Donkeys, and Mules

- To tame a horse, donkey, or mule try to ride the animal.
- The animal will most likely throw you off a few times.
- Once you see hearts, the animal has been trained, and you can sit on it, but you can't ride it or control it until it has been saddled.

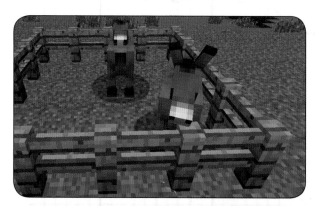

Step 7: Ocelots and Cats

Facts about Ocelots

- Are found naturally as ocelots and become one of three breeds of cats once tamed.
- Do not drop anything when killed.
- Found in jungle biomes.
- Will continue to follow a player and meow once tamed.
- Cause fear in creepers, who are afraid of cats and will run away if one is nearby; this makes them handy to have following you around.
- Are scared easily so are difficult to tame.
- Tame with raw fish.
- Breed with raw fish.
- Can be tamed if you can catch it on a lead, stake it to the ground, and wait nearby for it to beg for food.
- Can be ordered to sit and stay instead of follow you.

Taming Ocelots

- First, find an ocelot in a jungle.
- Have raw fish in hand.
- Find an ocelot and try to get close enough without scaring it away, then let it approach you.
- Will give off hearts and take on one of the cat skins once tamed.

Step 8: Wolves and Dogs

Facts about Wolves

- Are considered neutral mobs as they can be both passive and hostile.
- Does not drop anything when killed.
- Can be tamed by feeding bones.
- Can be bred using meat or rotten flesh.
- When tamed, a red collar will appear around the wolf's neck (it can be dyed another color).
- When a wolf is hostile, its tail will stick out straight and its eyes will be red; it will attack and kill sheep whenever it wants, but will only attack a player if it is attacked first.
- Once a wolf is tamed it will follow you around unless you tell it to sit/stay.
- A tamed wolf will attack whatever the player attacks (except creepers).

Step 9: Squids

Facts about Squids

- Will not attack you, even if you attack them.
- Are only found in water.
- Will drop ink sacs when killed, which can be used as black dye.

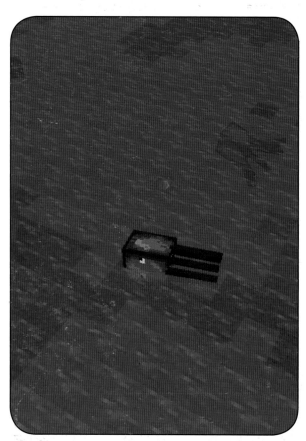

Step 10: Bats

Facts about Bats

- Bats are passive mobs.
- They will not attack you even if you attack or kill them.
- Do not drop anything when killed.
- Are found in caverns.
- Don't do anything except fly around and squeak in the dark.

How to Get Around

Nicole Smith

http://www.instructables.com/id/Getting-around-in-Minecraft/

There are a few ways to find your way around in the game. You can just wander around, keep track of your coordinates, craft up a boat, or even zoom around in a Minecart. Check out this collection of ways to find your way around in Minecraft.

Step 1: Coordinates

Coordinates are very handy for finding your way around, assuming you remember the coordinates of where you were so you can find your way back later. To see your coordinates, you need to pull up the Debug screen, which is done by hitting F3 on the computer version. The Debug screen gives you a lot of information, but we are going to concentrate on the coordinate-related points. The points are based on an origin point. What you are going to use from the Debug screen:

- X-coordinate: shows how far east (positive number) or west (negative number) you are
- Z-coordinate: shows how far south (positive number) or north (negative number) you are
- Y-coordinate: shows how above or below sea level (Level 63) you are (this does not go negative)
- Direction: you can tell what direction you are facing by looking at the f: number
  - 0 = South
  - 1 = West
  - 2 = North
  - 3 = East

- Biome: the b: tells you which biome you are in; the screenshot shows I am in "Plains".

Using Coordinates
- I find it most handy to record the X and Z of certain locations I want to keep in mind (home, lava pool, jungle, mooshroom biome, etc.).
- If you are able to walk exactly straight in one direction, only the X or Z coordinates will change; this is very difficult and most likely they will both change as you go.

Step 2: Maps

Maps are kind of troublesome to use. They are mostly handy for keeping track of one area of the game. When you create a map, you will be able to see yourself as a white arrow shape wandering around that map. If you leave the area of the map, you can create another map. On that map you will be able to see your white arrow shape. If you go back into the area of the first map, it will no longer work. Only your current map will show your exact location as you move around.

In order to use a map, you have to complete it. To complete it, hold your empty map like you would any resource and click to use it. You can watch as the map creates itself. Once it is active, the empty map icon will look the same, except it will have black squiggles on it. Each map you complete will have a number. Even if you delete a previous numbered map, the map numbers will continue to go up.

To cover more area on a single map, you can zoom out by combining it with more paper. You can zoom out a map four levels beyond your start level, meaning there are five levels the map can show. At the lowest level of the map everything will show up in a 1 to 1 scale. For each box on the map, it will be a box in the game.

Crafting:
- 3 Sugar Canes = 3 Pieces of Paper
- 4 Iron Ingots + 1 Redstone = 1 Compass
- 8 Pieces of Paper + 1 Compass = 1 Empty Map
- 8 Pieces of Paper + 1 Completed Map = 1 Zoomed Out Map
- Completed Map + Blank Map = Cloned Map

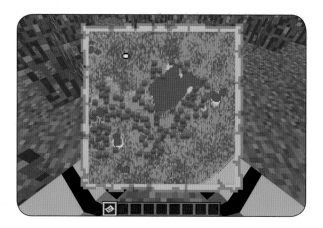

Step 3: Boats

Boats are amazing for covering great distances on water since they go faster than you can walk or swim. The downside to them is they are extremely fragile. You can destroy a boat by hitting a lily pad, hitting a squid, or just going too close to shore while going too fast. If you are boating near shore, it is wise to slow down.

A boat destroyed by crashing it will drop two sticks and three wood planks, unless you destroy a boat by hitting it, in which case it will drop a boat. When not riding in your boat, you are going to want to destroy it to get a boat, or "dock it." The best way to dock it is to get close to land, preferably with a side already blocked in. Then completely block it in on all sides. It should stay there. Do not dock a boat by digging into the shore, driving the boat into the hole you have created, and then blocking it in. If you do, the water will flow into the hole until you block it off, then it will stop flowing and you will get the boat stuck on land. You can get it back on water again, but it is easier to dock it in still water.

Crafting
• 5 Wood Planks = 1 Boat

Step 4: Rails and Minecarts

Rails and minecarts are very handy for use while mining in Minecraft, but they can also be used as transportation. To make them useful you are going to need to learn more about powered tracks. I talk about them in my Instructable "How to Mine in Minecraft," but I will cover them more here as well.

When using rails, you can use normal rails by themselves, but you have to direct them like when you walk, and they won't go very fast unless you are going downhill.

Common Trails of Redstone Rails
• Power with a redstone block, redstone torch, redstone in combination with a lever or button or redstone torch, or with just a lever or button; using a lever will turn the rail on and off, a button will turn it on temporarily, and a redstone torch will leave it on.
• Rails connected together will power one another if they are the same; i.e., an activated powered rail will activate any other powered rails it touches but will not power an activator or detector rail (this is not true with a detector rail, since its purpose is to power/activate other rails).
• Powered rails and activator rails will show up red when placed next to a redstone power source; a detector rail will show up red once activated by a minecart and so will the rail it activates.

Powered Rail
• Is most helpful of the special rails.
• Are used to speed up and stop minecarts: speed up when activated, stop when deactivated.
• Can be powered from above, below, or from any side.
• Combine with detector rails for one-way (one detector rail on one end of the powered rails) or two-way (one detector rail on each end of the powered rails) travel.
• Optimal spacing is 1 every 38 blocks, but this only works if the minecart has gathered speed; when the minecart first starts going they need to be closer, otherwise it won't reach the next powered rail. To get it started try not to space them more than eight or so regular rails apart (to figure out the spacing the best thing to do is just activate the powered rail with the minecart on it and just see how far it can go, then place a powered rail as far as you can so that it will still reach.

Detector Rail
• Is a pressure plate and can be used to activate redstone or powered rails.
• Is finicky on slopes.

Activator Rail
• Is used with special minecarts, such as those containing TNT or a hopper.

- When off acts like a normal rail, unlike a powered rail.
- When combined with a TNT minecart will light the TNT.
- When combined with a hopper minecart turns off the hopper.
- Ejects things in carts that go over it.

Crafting Minecarts
- 5 Iron Ingots in a "U" shape = Minecart
- Minecart + Chest = Minecart with Chest
- Minecart + Furnace = Minecart with Furnace
- Minecart + Hopper = Minecart with Hopper
- Minecart + TNT = Minecart with TNT

Crafting Rail
- 6 Iron Ingots + 1 Stick = 16 Rails
- 6 Gold Ingots + 1 Stick + 1 Redstone = 6 Powered Rails
- 6 Iron Ingots + 1 Stone Pressure Plate + 1 Redstone = 6 Detector Rails
- 6 Iron Ingots + 1 Redstone Torch + 2 Sticks = 6 Activator Rails

Other Supplies
- 1 Stick + 1 Block of Cobblestone = 1 Lever
- 1 Stone + 1 Wooden Plank = 1 Button

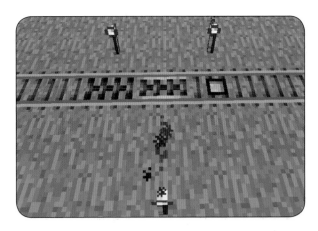

Fun Structures

Castle

Steve's RV

Steve's Yacht

Archery Range

Prison Tower

Glass Dome

Fishing House

Castle

Kurtis

(http://www.instructables.com/id/Castle/)

Step 1: The Base

First, find a big area to build on. Then build the front and back sides of the castle 21 blocks long. The two sides are 16 blocks long. Now fill in the square you have made.

Step 2: Making the Towers

Make the walls 3 x 3 and make the tower 8 blocks tall, making sure there is an entrance if you want. Repeat this for each corner.

Step 3: Now Make the Top

To make the tower look better, make an extension one block out (5 x 5) and do the ledges as I have shown.

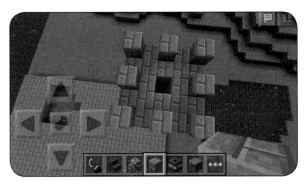

Step 4: Make Three More Towers

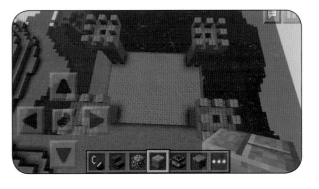

Step 5: Build the Walls

Make the walls five blocks high. This is probably the easiest step!

Step 6: Now the Roof

You can do the roof however you like. I put in glow stone so that you can see inside the castle.

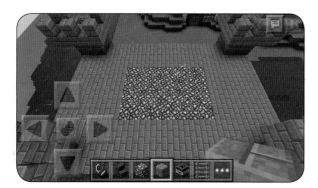

Step 7: Decorate

Now make the inside look amazing!

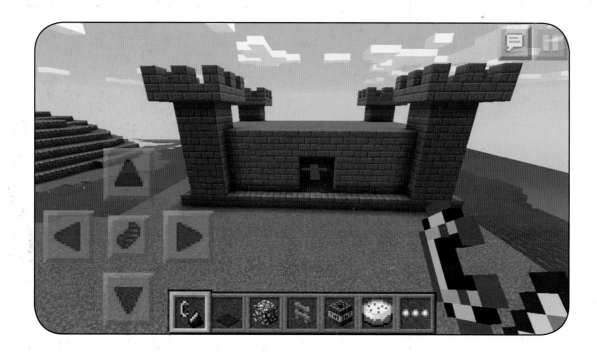

Steve's RV

shankybatra

(http://www.instructables.com/id/minecraft-
steves-RV/)

Step 1: Build the Wheel

Take any black block and lay four of them on the plane. Build a tire and put a clay block in it for the wheel.

Step 2: Another Wheel

Make a horizontal block bar and build another wheel.

Step 3: Mirror It

Now build a mirror copy of your structure and join them.

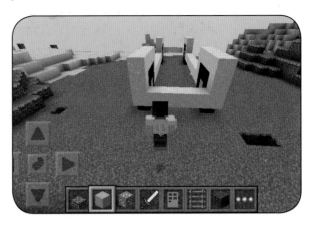

Step 4: Go Inside and Start Building

Now start building the body of RV from within. First clear any extra blocks.

Step 5: Exteriors

Go outside the RV and start building the exterior. Put the doors on too.

Step 6: Interiors

Now go inside and build the floor of the RV in fly mode. Finally, put the glass in for windows, front and back. Now place beds in the back of the RV.

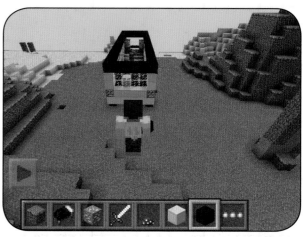

Step 7: Add Comfort

Build a sofa using stairs and tiles. When interiors are done, put some torches or lamps in for light.

Step 9: Add a Rooftop

Now add a rooftop and it's done.

Step 8: Add Some Features

Use jack-o-lanterns for headlights and indicators.

Steve's Yacht

shankybatra
(http://www.instructables.com/id/minecraft-steves-yatch/)

Step 1: Base

To build a yacht you will need a large plane of land. Build a base as shown in pictures. Now start building the structure, also shown in the pictures. The lowest part of your yacht is done.

Step 2: First Floor

Extend the walls and build a small room, then extend the roof of the room to cover whole yacht.

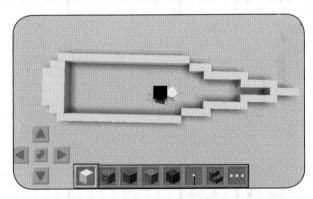

Step 3: Second Floor

Now build the second floor.

43

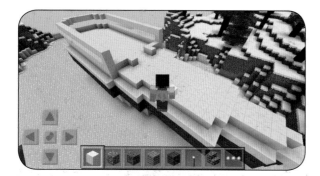

Step 4: Stairs

Build stairs from first floor to top floor.

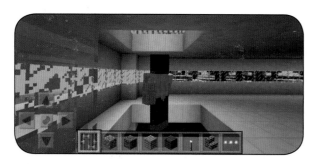

Step 5: Pool

Build a pool on the second floor.

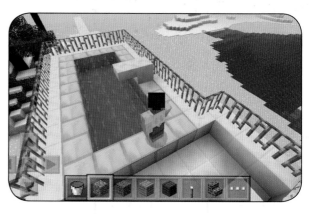

Step 6: Secret Base

Build TNT storage down in the base.

Step 7: Water

Fill with water using water bucket.

Step 8: Captain's Cabin and Dock

Build a cabin for the captain and then a dock. Enjoy!

Archery Range

Shroomers

(http://www.instructables.com/id/Archery-Range-Minecraft-Pe/)

In this Instructable, I'm going to be showing you how to make an archery range!

Step 1: Materials
- Fences
- Flint and steel
- Netherack
- Bedrock (or another type of stone)
- Stone
- Stone walls

Step 2: The Post
Place the fences on top of each other for the desired height.

Step 3: The Target
Place the netherack on top of the fences to make the target.

Step 4: Flaming Target
If you would like your target to have fire on it, click on the top of the netherack with your flint and steel.

Step 5: The Fences
Use the stone fences to make a boundary around the target. (Just copy the picture.)

Step 6: The Floor
Use the stone (or any other block) to make the flooring. Add one more different type of block where you want people to stand when shooting.

Step 7: Finishing it up
Now, just make as many as you want! I made five more at different heights.

If you use fire, the fire will catch the fences on fire. I suggest using stone fences instead!

Prison Tower

NVDevastator

(http://www.instructables.com/id/Minecraft-Prison-Towers/)

These are two simple prison towers (or call them whatever you like). Feel free to edit them however you like. Let us begin, shall we?

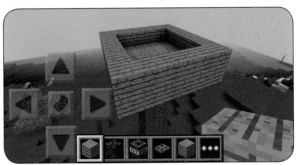

Step 1: Tower 1

For this tower you need 141 wood planks, 40 glass blocks, 9 wood stairs, 2 ladders, 4 torches, and a trapdoor. Make a 2 x 2 square and build it 12 block lengths high. On top of that make a 6 x 6 square. Now make a ring around the outside. Add glass on top of that two blocks up. Make a roof. Now wrap stairs around the center of the pole the holds up the tower. Once you get to where you can't go up anymore, put the ladders on the wall and add a trap door on top of the hole. Now you're done!

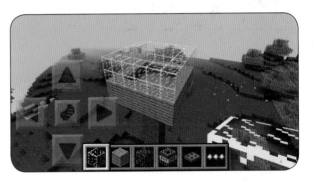

Step 2: Tower 2

In my opinion, this is the best looking tower of the two. It's more modern as well. For this tower you'll need 198 wood planks, 96 glass blocks, 19 wood stairs, 2 ladders, a door, and some torches. Make a 4 x 4 square without corners and build it 12 block lengths high. Leave space for a door. Make a floor. Make the wood blocks so they only touch on the corner of the block, so they don't touch on top or on the side; they should only touch on the corner. It will stick one block length away from the floor. Do this one more time (still going away) with glass. Build the glass 3 blocks high on top of each other. Now reverse the corner-touch to go inward. (Refer to the pictures. They will help you a lot.) Do this one more time inward and fill in the roof. Add stairs inside. (See pictures to see how to do this.) Once you can't go up any higher, break the block above you and add two ladders going up. Place torches on the inside so it doesn't become a monster spawner. Now you have a prison/watch tower! Hope you like it!

Step 3: Or. . .

You can replace the glass with a fence to give it a maximum-security-prison effect!

Glass Dome

Jacob Rees

(http://www.instructables.com/id/How-To-Make-A-Glass-Dome-On-Minecraft/)

Warning: This set of instructions is intended for intermediate and experienced Minecraft players. If you are not an experienced Minecraft player you will need to follow the in-game instructions to learn how to play the game in order to be able to follow these instructions. This set of instructions is a guide on how to construct a glass dome in Minecraft. A glass dome in Minecraft is a pixelated dome meant to resemble a real-life dome. Since Minecraft is strictly square, the dome will not be spherical, but it will resemble a curved, spherical dome as shown in the figure below. This process could take from a few minutes to a few hours depending on the size of your dome and how skilled you are at Minecraft.

Step 1: Materials

In order to start building the dome you will need the following materials (Fig. 1 shows an example of these materials):

- You will need a certain number of glass blocks depending on the size of your dome.
- You will need one 64-piece stack of dirt blocks.

These are the only materials you will need unless you have not yet made glass. In that case, you will need the following materials (Fig. 2 shows an example of these materials):

- You will need a certain number of sand blocks depending on the size of your dome.
- You will need coal or charcoal, specifically an eighth of the amount of sand you are using.

Step 2: Sizing and Flattening

In order to start building your dome you will need to choose a size for it. The chart below shows the blueprint of valid dome sizes in Minecraft that you can choose from. Once you have selected the size of the dome you will need to clear sufficient space. This simply requires making a flat surface in your Minecraft world big enough to hold the diameter of your dome. Once you have done that you will need to follow the chart below in order to outline the bottom of your dome with glass.

Note: In order to avoid wasting glass blocks use dirt blocks to outline the dome and when you know that the outline is correct you can replace the dirt blocks with glass blocks.

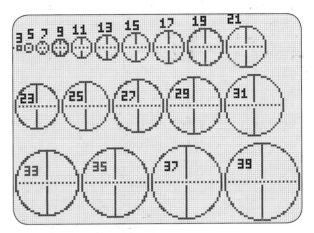

Step 3: Construction

At this point in the process you will need to either have all the glass required to make the dome or you will need to continuously make glass by burning sand in a furnace and using coal or charcoal as fuel for the furnace. Now you can start to construct the dome. You will need to reference the chart in the last step for this. You will need to construct a half circle going vertically into the air at the points where the cross in the chart touches the circle on both sides. This will complete the outline of your dome. The figure below shows a small example.

Note: The size of the half circle is half of the size of the dome you choose.

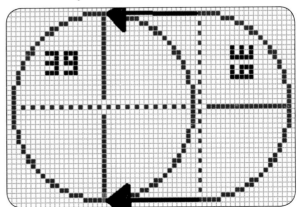

49

Step 4: Adding Height

Next you're going to add blocks to the perimeter of your dome. The number of blocks you add is based on the size dome you have chosen. For a size 39 dome you will add 4 blocks; for a size 21 dome you will add 3 blocks. The figure below gives a visual example. In order for you to figure out the number of blocks you are supposed to place vertically, you have to cut the outline of the dome in half and take the number of blocks from where the cross hits the circle to the point where the blocks shift over. Once you know how to do this the rest of the dome should be fairly easy to complete.

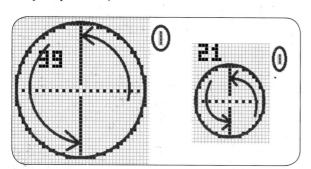

Step 5: Completion

After learning the previous step all you have to do is repeat it, except you follow the outline and push in one block for each layer of glass and reduce your wall vertically to match the dome outline that you made in step 3. Do this until the dome is completely finished. The figure below shows the best representation of this process.

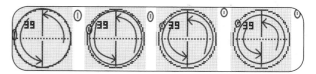

Step 6: Conclusion

Finally, your glass dome should be complete, and it should look something like the figure below. It may be smaller or larger depending on the size you chose for your dome. I hope these instructions have helped you in the process of making a glass dome on Minecraft.

Fishing House
NVDevastator
(http://www.instructables.com/id/Minecraft-Fishing-House/)

You'll need wood blocks, 4 fences, 4 torches, 1 chest, 1 bed, and 1 furnace. This can be modified to make it bigger or smaller or thinner, etc. Do what you want with it!

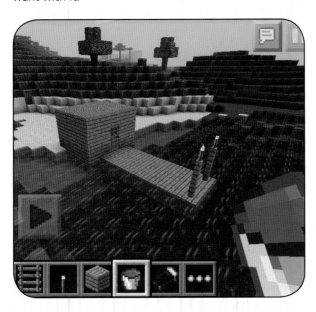

Step 1: Base
For this you'll need 43 wood blocks. First make a 5 x 5 square and add a 3 x 6 across the water.

Step 2: House
On the 5 x 5 square, add walls as high as you want as well as a roof. Inside you can put a bed, furnace,

crafting table, chest, or whatever you want. Also add a torch or two inside. Add doors.

Step 3: Almost There!
Now at the end of the plank add 2 fence posts on each side and top with torches.

Step 4: Done
Now you have an awesome fishing house. Have fun!

Unique Objects

How to Make a Fireplace That Won't Burn Your House Down

Nicole Smith

http://www.instructables.com/id/How-to-make-a-Fireplace-that-wont-burn-your-House-/

Fireplaces are great decorative pieces for your house in Minecraft, but if you are not careful, you can end up burning down your beautiful home. Though the overall look of your fireplace is up to you, here is what you need to know to ensure you don't burn your house down (unless it is made of a nonflammable material, in which case you are already fine).

- Decide where it is going to go (I chose the corner of my house).
- Clear out the area you want it in.
  - Ensure the area under the fire is made of nonflammable material.
  - Clear one block in each direction around where the fire will be, or make sure it is a nonflammable material, so a 3 x 3 square around it.
  - Going up from where the fire will be, you will need that 3 x 3 square to be made of nonflammable material for at least three levels above it. The only way to ensure nothing starts on fire is to keep that 3 x 3 rectangle made of nonflammable material no matter how far up you go from the fire; either have the material above it be nonflammable or have nothing there (you can see the picture of the roof of my house where I continued the 3 x 3 block of stone.

- Fill in stone (or another nonflammable material) around where the fireplace will be (anywhere the fire could touch), which includes below and above as directed earlier.
- Create a boundary around what will be on fire (I used stone steps, leaving a hole in the corner where my fire source will be).
- Cover the area that will be above the fire with stone so it doesn't light up (as long as you just leave a one-block-high opening around where the fire will be, you will not be in danger of getting burned because you will physically not be able to touch it).
- Put your flammable material in the fireplace (I just chose to use a block of wood, which actually burned for quite some time).
- Light it on fire with flint and steel.

There you have it! Make sure the fire doesn't spread, and enjoy!

How to Make Golems

Nicole Smith

http://www.instructables.com/id/Making-Golems-in-Minecraft/

Minecraft golems can help you attack and defend against enemies. There are two types: snow golems and iron golems.

Step 1: Snow Golem
Facts about Snow Golems
- Created by stacking 2 snow blocks with 1 pumpkin on top.
- Will drop a few snowballs when destroyed.
- Leaves a trail of snow wherever it walks, which can then be harvested for more snowballs.
- Attacks enemies by throwing snowballs, but this does not do any damage to them (except for blazes, but snow golems don't do well in the Nether), mostly distracts the monsters so you can attack and kill them.
- Will be damaged by water; rain quickly kills it.
- Take damage in hot biomes such as deserts, savannah, jungles, and mesas.
- Won't attack creepers or hostile wolves.

Step 2: Iron Golem
Facts about Iron Golems
- Created by stacking 2 iron blocks and putting 1 iron block on either side of the top iron block, then top it with a pumpkin.
- Can appear naturally in villages and will protect the villagers, will stay near a village if naturally spawned there or if you created one there.
- Attacks by swinging its arms and hitting enemies.
- Can pick up and will give poppies to villagers.
- Won't attack creepers
- Naturally occurring Iron Golems will attack you if you attack them
- Will only drop a few Iron Ingots and Poppies when killed

Step 3: Tether and Lead
Golems tend to just wander around if you make them and let them do what they want to do. To keep them nearby you can either lead them around with a lead, tether them to a post with a lead, or even block them in with a fence. Be careful about putting them next to each other, as the iron golem can hit anything nearby and will kill your snow golems with one hit. It is better to keep them away from each other.
Crafting
- 9 Iron Ingots = 1 Iron Block
- 4 Snowballs = 1 Block of Snow

How to Make a Realistic Man-made Lake

~KnexBuild~

(http://www.instructables.com/id/How-to-make-a-realistic-man-made-lake-in-Minecraft/)

In this Instructable I will show how to build a man-made lake in Minecraft. Let's get started, shall we?

Step 1: Explosives

Place some TNT on the ground. TNT makes a realistic lake because it always produces a random crater.

Step 2: Filling in One Layer

Fill in the second-from-the-top layer of the hole. Don't fill it up underneath; just leave it hollow.

Step 3: Adding Water and Sand

Add some sand around the perimeter of the lake. This makes it more realistic. Next, add some water. Make sure that it is completely flat with no currents.

Step 4: Breaking the Dirt Layer

Swim in the water and break the dirt layer that you made. The water will flow in completely and there will be no currents.

Step 5: You're Done!

You're done building your man-made lake.

57

Trash Can
NVDevastator
(http://www.instructables.com/id/Cool-and-Simple-Minecraft-trash-can/)

Ever get something you don't want in your chest but you don't want it sitting around for five minutes? Then you need a cactus trash can! It really works! Works on PC or PE (Pocket Edition)! Let's go!

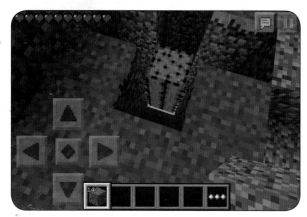

Step 1
Dig three blocks down to make a + sign, but dig four down in the middle. Put a block of sand there. Put two cacti on the sand. It should be one block from the surface.

Step 2
Fill in only the top of the plus except on top of the cactus (duh). Put one block behind and put a trap door over it.

Step 3: Done
Now you've got an awesome (and legit) trash can! Enjoy throwing away unneeded items!

How to Make a Cool Bunk Bed

cdog557

(http://www.instructables.com/id/How-To-Make-A-Cool-Bunk-Bed/)

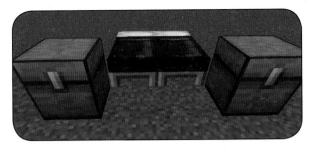

Step 4: Fences

Fill in the space between the chests with fencing and then put it on the chests.

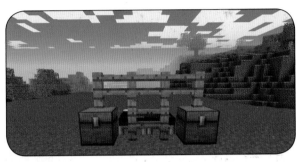

Step 5: Wooden Blocks and Tiles

Put the wooden blocks on one side of the bed and the wooden tile on the other side.

Step 1: Find Space

Load up a new world and find a good flat space or find a good place in your house.

Step 2: Beds

Put two beds down side by side.

Step 6: Ladders

Put ladders on the wooden blocks.

Step 7: Bookshelves

Put bookshelves in a 4 block by 3 block in a square.

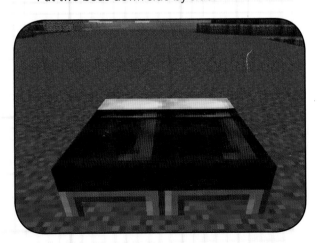

Step 3: Chests

Put two chests beside the beds.

Step 8: Top

Cover the top with wooden blocks.

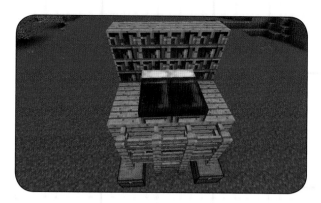

Step 11: Finish It Off

Put more fences where the tile is. Add more chests on the edges of the fences. Finish it off by putting tile on top of the bookshelves as show in the image.

Step 9: Delete Wooden Blocks

Delete wooden blocks except the ones with the ladders, then put wooden tiles where the blocks were.

Step 10: More Beds

Put two beds side by side and put more bookshelves above it.

Wrestling Ring

JLAwesomeness2468

(http://www.instructables.com/id/Minecraft-Wrestling-Ring/)

Step 1: Building the Frame

First, you take a red wool block and make an 8x8 square two blocks high.

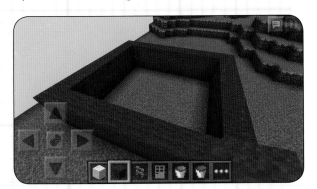

Step 2: The Mat

I used white wool for this, but you can use whatever you want.

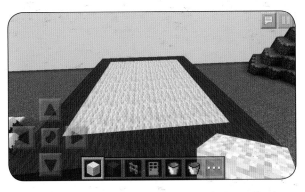

Step 3: The Ropes

For the ropes I used wood fence, but you can use the cobblestone wall or anything similar.

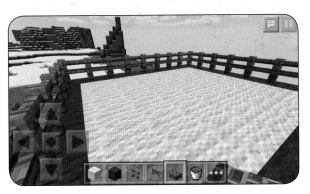

Step 4: The Steps

For the steps just use any kind of slab; I used brick.

Step 5: Voila!

And you're done. You can have death matches in survival mode with it, which is really fun.

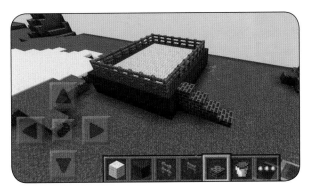

Basketball Court

tkauffman2

(http://www.instructables.com/id/Minecraft-Basketball-Court/)

Step 3: Hoop

Make a backboard and hoop. Start by stacking fences 2 wide and 5 high. No top of that make a 3 by 3 square of wood planks. Sticking out of the bottom center wooden plank, add three fences in the shape of a hoop as shown.

Step 4: Lines

To add on the courts lines replace some of the wooden planks with white and red wool (or any material you want).

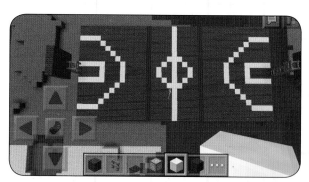

Step 1: Space

Have a lot of space.

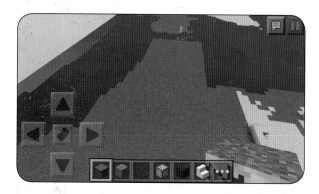

Step 2: Court

Put the blocks down as large as you want it. "I made mine 18 x 37 squares."

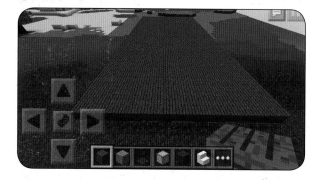

Stargate

Transforminglegodude

http://www.instructables.com/id/Minecraft-Stargate/

Step 1: The Base

Dig out a 3 x 5 space and fill with quartz.

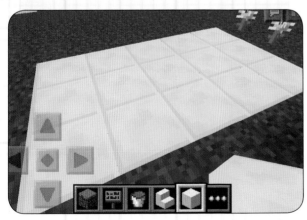

Step 2: The Frame

Place stairs and blocks of a material of choice as shown in the pictures (Quartz Stairs and Quarts Blocks are shown here). Also place a sign at each side. One should say "to Earth" and the other "to Mars".

Step 3: Finishing

Remember the holes in the roof? Fill them with water.

Hot Tub
NVDevastator
(http://www.instructables.com/id/Minecraft-Hot-Tub/)

This is a hot tub that will need 9 glowstones, 9 glass, 9 buckets of water, 48 wooden or stone slabs (you can also use 16 wood/stone blocks for the base instead of slabs). The glowstone and glass are optional but look cool.

Note: This works in Pocket Edition now.

Step 1: Beginning

Dig a 3 x 3 x 3 hole with a 5 x 5 x 1 ring around the outside of the highest block dug in. Fill the bottom with glowstone. Fill above that with glass. Fill the outside of the 5 x 5 square with wood or rock and fill with water.

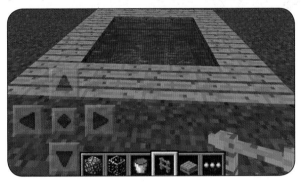

Step 2: Middle

Add a fence around the perimeter, setting it on the wood or rock, on all except one side. On the corners, build up three fence lengths up. On top of the fence lengths, put a slab. Make a 9 x 9 square (the exact same length/width as the hot tub itself) in the middle. In the very middle add a block and on the sides of it add slabs (see pictures).

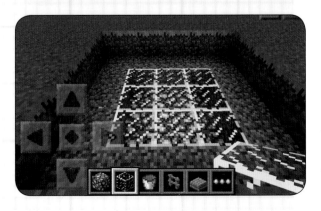

Step 3: The End
Now you have an awesome hot tub!

Obsidian Generator

Razorblade360

(http://www.instructables.com/id/Minecraft-
Obsidian-Generator/)

This is a Minecraft obsidian generator that works in all versions of Minecraft.

It's also reusable!

The pictures and instructions are for a generator that makes six obsidian.

Step 1: Materials

- 1 bucket of water for each obsidian block you intend to make
- At least 1 additonal bucket of water
- Approximately 50 fireproof blocks of your choice
- A lot of flat land

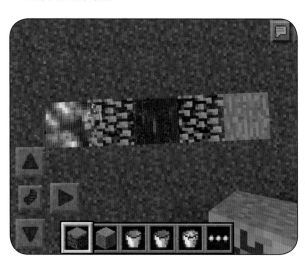

Step 2: Water Holder

This will work in almost any size, as long as it contains water. One block high will do. I made mine higher so I could put a cobblestone floor in it.

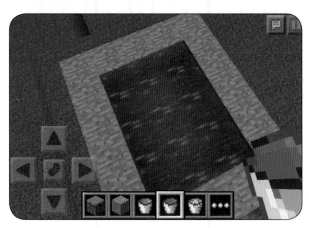

Step 3: Lava Holder

This needs to be right next to the water holder, with only one row of blocks separating the two.

It also needs to be a block lower than the water holder, so the water gets to the lava first.

I made a step between the lava and water holders on the lava side so the water has a place to run.

The lava holder needs to be two blocks deep so the lava has a higher wall around it.

Note: You need to place the lava one a square; for example, if I wanted to make 6 obsidian, I would make the lava holder two blocks wide and three blocks long—a six block space—and I would put one bucket of lava in each block space, to make six blocks.

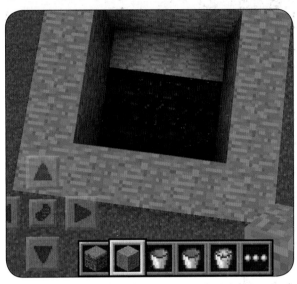

Step 4: Usage

To use, destroy one of the blocks separating the water from the step. If done correctly, the water will flow over the lava, turning it into obsidian. Now block off the water and you will be able to mine out the Obsidian you just created. I hope this works for you.

How to Make a Portal to the Nether

Keltonthebeast

(http://www.instructables.com/id/How-to-make-a-Minecraft-Portal-to-the-Nether/)

I know that a lot of people love Minecraft but have no idea how to make a Nether portal! Here's how to do that!

Step 1: Materials
- 14 obsidian blocks
- Flint and steel

Step 2: How to Make It!

Make a frame with obsidian 4 long and 5 high. Take your flint and steel and light the obsidian.

A blue light should appear inside; walk through that and you're in the nether.

Minecraft IRL

Chocolate Chip Cookies

looop45

(http://www.instructables.com/id/Minecraft-Chocolate-Chip-Cookies-IRL/)

There are a lot of Minecraft "in real life" (IRL) foods out there, but surprisingly no cookies. I had to do something about this monstrosity. I went straight to work planning out the idea. The recipe is really simple and can be done in almost no time at all. It's perfect for when you and your buddies decide to do a Minecraft all-nighter and need some chow. These cookies look amazing and taste just as good. It isn't that complicated to make, so please don't just look at the pictures.

Step 1: Ingredients

- 1 cup of shortening
- 3/4 cup white sugar
- 3/4 cup brown sugar
- 2 eggs
- 2 tsp. vanilla
- 1 tsp. salt
- 3/4 tsp. baking powder (has to be baking powder)
- 1/4 tsp. baking soda (use these exact measurements)
- 2 3/4 to 3 cups flour
- A handful of chocolate chips

This is just your regular old chocolate chip cookie recipe, but modified a little bit. We need to use baking powder and more flour than usual to make a stiffer, crispier dough that works like sugar cookie dough or Play-Doh. This way we can mold them into the iconic pixel shape. Don't skimp out on anything or it won't turn out right. This makes around 8 cookies, 10 if you are careful.

Step 2: Preheat the Oven

Preheat your oven to 350° F. Don't forget this step or else it takes a billion times longer.

Step 3: It's Creaming Time

In a large mixing bowl, cream together the shortening and both types of sugar. Cream until light and fluffy. Once fluffy, add both eggs one at a time, mixing continuously. This is the "egg goop part." We are preparing the wet side of the cookies so that when we add the dry side we have cookies with a better texture and a better taste, and we always want the better taste.

Step 4: Dry Stuff

In a separate bowl, lightly mix together the flour, baking soda and powder, and salt. This step isn't completely necessary to do but it does make the cookies more even, with no chunks or anything.

Step 5: Two Worlds Collide

Slowly add portions of the dry goods into the mixing bowl and mix on low; unless you want a brand new ghost costume, keep it on LOW! When you mix all the stuff together it will look a little crumbly, but trust yourself—if you did all the instructions right it will even out and become moist and delicious. DON'T ADD CHOCOLATE CHIPS!

Step 6: You Get to Play with Your Food!

Take the dough out of the bowl and put it on a clean, flat surface. Get a sizable hunk and flatten it out to about 1/3 of an inch in a kind of oval or circle shape. Use a butter knife to make a cut across the top and bottom. Now on all four corners cut away a little L shape to give it that pixel type look. Be sure to have slightly exaggerated edges, as the dough will puff out a little bit in cooking. At this point you can place your chocolate chips upside-down in the cookie; if you have chocolate chunks then even better. Now it looks like it does in the game.

Step 7: Give It to the Furnace!

Carefully move the cookies to a lined sheet pan and then place into the preheated oven. Keep these cookies in the furnace for around 8–10 minutes depending on how crispy you want them.

Step 8: Hold Right Click and Enjoy!

You are done. Let cool for a good 10 minutes though or else they will fall apart. Now you have a delicious cookie fit for a real gamer nerd or just the casual player. Give them to your friends, family, monkey, neighborhood hobo, or creeper—everybody loves them! Just be sure to wrap them in plastic wrap before you store them in your chest for eternity.

Character Cookies

Janine Eshelbrenner

(http://www.instructables.com/id/Minecraft-Cookies/)

If your kids love Minecraft, they'll flip over these Minecraft cookies!

Step 1: How to Make Minecraft Pig Cookies

- Cookies made from your favorite sugar cookie recipe and cut using a square cookie cutter
- Icing made from your favorite royal icing recipe in dark pink, medium pink, light pink, black, and white (I used 12-count consistency icing for all the steps in this tutorial. If you need help with icing color or consistency, check out the How To Make Royal Icing section of 101 Essential Cookie Decorating Resources.)
- A food coloring marker in any color
- Icing bags or bottles, couplers, and tips (I used a #2 tip for all the steps in this tutorial.)

Step 2: Create a Grid

Start by using a food coloring marker to draw straight lines, breaking each cookie up into eight rows and eight columns. This will give you 64 squares to fill with icing.

Using your printed template as a guide, fill in all of the squares labeled with the #1 with black royal icing. Before icing, you may want to mark the squares with your food coloring marker to help prevent mistakes. Complete this step on all of your pig Minecraft cookies and let the icing dry somewhat before moving on to the next color.

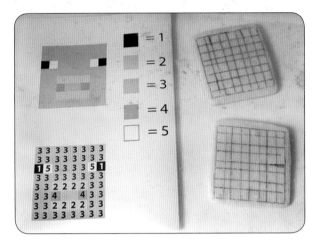

Step 3: More Colors

Repeat these steps for each of the additional four colors you are using on your pig cookies. Let the royal icing dry completely (preferably overnight) before stacking or packaging your cookies.

3-D Papercraft Terrains
laboratory424

(http://www.instructables.com/id/Build-3-D-
Papercraft-Terrains-Minecraft-Style/)

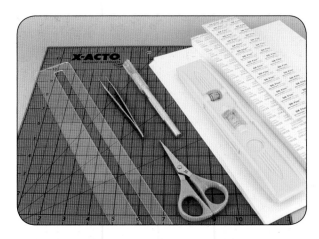

Some gamers need a Railgun, others choose an M1A1, most seem to desire an Energy Sword...but what we need is a pickaxe! That's right, our current favorite diversion from lab work is Minecraft. We didn't want the fun to stop on the screen, so we created giant, 3-D, papercraft Minecraft terrains on our walls. Here we will show you how to build your own. Enjoy.

NOTE: "Minecraft" is a trademark of Notch Development AB. The Minecraft block graphics are Copyright Mojang AB. Laboratory 424 is not affiliated with, nor endorsed by Mojang AB.

This Instructable shows you how to build giant 3-D Minecraft terrains on your wall using simple, raised papercraft panels. The papercraft panels use a modified version of our Panel Poster panels. They are fast to build, no glue is needed, and are easy to install and remove using our non-permanent adhesive blocks. Buy scoring, assembly, and mounting materials to build your own terrains.

Step 1: Get Tools and Materials
- Hobby knife
- Scissors
- Self-healing mat (or similar)
- Tweezers (optional)
- Small level (optional)
- Sheets of 110 lb, 8.5" x 11" (216mm x 279mm) card stock (or similar)
- 1 Panel Poster Starter Pack (includes score tool and adhesive)
- Panel Poster Adhesive Packs

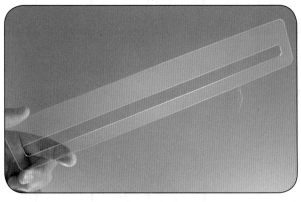

Step 2: Design
Measure the area you are installing on. Each panel is 2 x 2 inches (5.08 x 5.08 cm), so divide your

width and length measurements by 2 (or 5.08) to get the maximum number of blocks you'll need in both directions. Now fire up Minecraft and make your epic terrain.

Step 3: Download & Print

Itemize the different Minecraft blocks used in your design. Download a panel template for each type of block.

For each type of block, count the number of individual blocks you need, divide by 6 (there are 6 panels per page), and round up. That's how many copies you need. Print them on card stock. Make sure you do not scale the graphic in your print settings. It should print at its actual size.

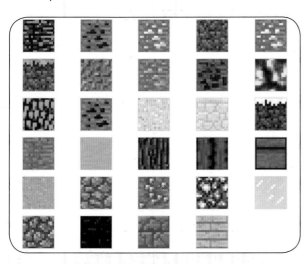

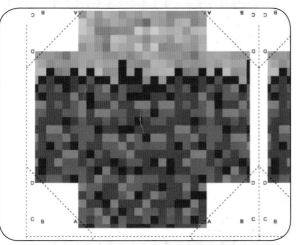

Step 4: Score

The key to quickly creating a perfect panel is using our Panel Poster Score Guide to make a clean edge perfectly spaced to produce the proper panel height for installation. However, if you do not want to purchase a score guide, you can use a ruler and space your score lines 1/2" (1.27 cm) apart.

1. Place a page on the cutting mat, face up. Position inside of score guide along one edge of the panels and hold firmly in place.
2. Using the back edge of a hobby knife, drag a score line along the inside edge of the score guide. Keep the knife at a sharp angle and apply pressure during the process.
3. Score with back edge of hobby knife along the outside edge of guide.
4. Repeat for the other three edges along the same orientation.
5. Rotate the paper and repeat for the other six edges.

Step 5: Cut

1. Using the hobby knife and score guide, cut along the five dashed lines on the page to separate the panels.
2. Cut lines A and B, stopping at line D. Repeat for all four corners.
3. Cut line C, stopping at line A. Cut line D, stopping at line B. Repeat for all four corners.
4. Cut the corner off from the end of line A to the end of line D. Repeat for all four corners.

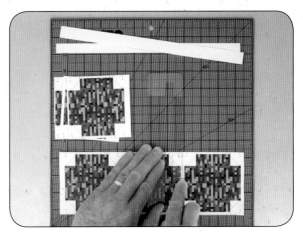

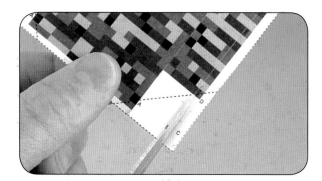

3. Peel away the protective cover on the block. Place the panel over the block with a level on the panel, and adjust the panel until it is level. Apply light pressure while rubbing your finger around the foam block to bond it to the paper.

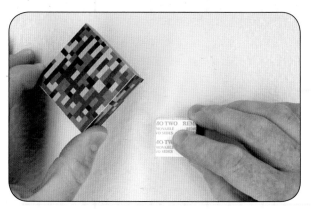

Step 6: Assemble

1. Flip the panel over and fold all score lines and tabs inward.
2. Using the hobby knife and score guide, cut the double-stick tape strips in half. Place a tape strip opposite each tab so the tape is close to the cut edge and between the score lines.
3. Remove the protective sheets from the tape. Line up a corner so the edges are even and apply pressure to the tab against the tape to set the corner. Repeat for all four corners.
4. Fold the outer edges so they point inward but do not stick to the tape.

Step 7: Install First Panel

Print out a screenshot of your Minecraft design. Choose the location where you want to install it. The adhesive-block backing has a rubber-based, non-permanent adhesive that can bond and be removed cleanly from all sorts of surfaces. We don't recommend installing on wallpaper. Wipe down the surface with a lint-free cloth to remove dust. You should level/square the first panel on the wall since all the other panels are aligned to it. The rest of the panels go up very quickly.

1. Remove an adhesive block from the sheet, place the panel on the wall, and hold the block over the approximate center of the panel.
2. Pull the panel away and press the block onto the spot you chose. Apply firm pressure for 10 seconds while rocking your thumb back and forth to bond with the surface.

Step 8: Install Next Panel

Get another adhesive block from the sheet and your next panel to install.
1. Position the panel next to the previous panel. Hold the block over the approximate center of the panel.
2. Pull the panel away and press the block onto the spot you chose. Apply firm pressure for 10 seconds while rocking your thumb back and forth to bond with the surface. Peel away the protective cover on the block.
3. Orient the panel in the same direction as the first one. Place the panel over the block and align the edges with the previous panel. Apply gentle, lateral pressure so the edges of each panel touch and close the gap nicely. Once aligned, gently apply pressure while rubbing your finger around the foam block to bond it to the paper.

Step 9: Install the Rest

The rest of the panels are very easy to install. You simply align the next panel with the previous, and so on. Repeat Step 8 for the rest of the panels. Do not worry about slight imperfections in panel-to-panel alignment. It isn't noticeable in most installations. Enjoy.

Notes: If a panel is damaged, simply build another panel, remove the damaged panel, and install the new panel. You can reuse the adhesive foam blocks if desired. Each panel's surface is designed to curve slightly inward. Learn more. If this is a problem, we recommend using Panel Poster Extensions to reduce the curvature of the panels.

Pickax Lamp

John G.

(http://www.instructables.com/id/How-to-Make-a-Minecraft-Pickaxe-Lamp/)

Today I am going to be showing you how to make a Pickax Lamp. Hope you enjoy my Instructable!

Step 1: Materials

- Around 70 wooden 3/4th in. cubes
- Gorilla glue
- Acrylic paints
- A Minecraft pickaxe sprite printed off the Internet
- A 13" x 13" shadow box
- 2 LED headlamp things
- A lot of time and patience

Step 2: Time to Paint!

Get your paints and your sprite. Start by figuring out which pixels are on the edge. These pixels will have to be painted on more than one side. Then, go to town mixing paints and painting your cubes on their respective sides for assembly.

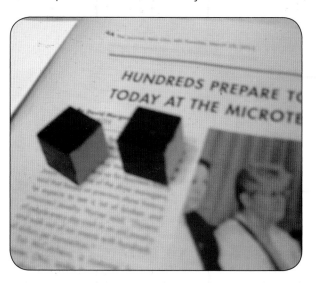

Step 3: Time to Glue!

Now that your cubes are painted start to assemble them to look like a pickax. Start by gluing them in stripes of 3 blocks. You can see below how you will have a bunch of lines of three blocks which will then be glued together. Once the strips of three blocks are dry, glue those lines of three blocks to each other.

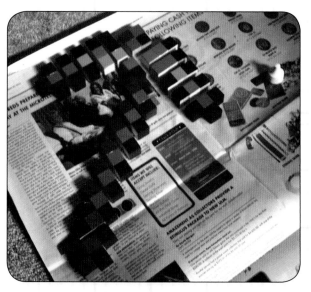

Step 4: Done Gluing!

Once the other pieces are dry, glue the rest of it together to form the correct shape! And you're done with the glue! Almost. . .

also used the Dremel to cut notches in the side of the shadow box so I could slip the wires to the LEDs in the sides. After that, pop the batteries in the headlamps and you're ready to turn it on! It looks really awesome in the dark!

Step 7: You're Done!

Yay! You've completed my Instructable! I hope you enjoyed it, and I hope the process of getting it together went well.

Step 5: Assembly

Get a paper background and glue it to the back of the shadow box. Then, hot glue your assembled pickaxe inside the box on the paper background.

Step 6: Final Touches

I took apart the headlamps to get at what we want, the LEDs. I used a Dremel to cut the headlamps about in half, being careful to avoid the parts inside. I

Creeper Wedding Cake Toppers

Laura-Jo Gartside

(http://www.instructables.com/id/Minecraft-Creeper-Wedding-Cake-Toppers/)

Are you a creeper who is getting married soon and struggling to find cake toppers that really represent you and your beloved? Then this is the Instructable for you! Alternatively, you may also like it if you are just a huge fan of the iconic Minecraft villain and want to celebrate your geek/gamer pedigree on your big day.

Step 1: Ingredients
- Liquid latex
- Epoxy resin (or any two-part resin mixing kit from a craft store)
- Measuring cup (usually comes with resin)
- Paper cup, with a pouring spout pinched into it
- Paintbrush (one that is cheap enough to throw away afterwards, but not so cheap that bristles will come out at the slightest pressure)
- Regular drinking/shot glass with water in it
- Superglue
- Tissue blade or fine craft knife
- Kitchen paper towel
- 20g black polymer clay
- 60g scrap polymer clay (any color)
- Latex gloves
- Fine-colored ribbon, 3–4mm wide. The ones found inside clothes to help you hang them are perfect
- Miniature ribbon rose
- Gauze, 3cm x 3cm
- Scissors
- 5g black seed beads
- 130–150g mixed green seed beads
- Chopstick, wooden skewer, or similar item for stirring resin mix.

The green seed beads should be in a color mix that is as close to the creeper's color mix as possible. I strongly suggest walking into a craft store and handling a few tubes next to each other to get a good idea of how they catch the light and would blend together. This is especially important because—as we all know—browsers represent colors differently, website photography may be not be top notch, and different ways of finishing the beads (silver lined, transparent, rainbow) can affect the overall impression.

The good news is you don't have to get high-quality beads for this, as they won't be strung or woven. Essentially, if you're happy with the color, that is enough. However, to avoid any nasty surprises you may wish to set 3–4 of your chosen beads in a teaspoon of resin as a tester to see if there is any discoloration or leakage.

Step 2: Making the Master
Wearing the latex gloves, roll your scrap polymer clay into something that is approximately 9.5cm.

Cut off 3cm with the tissue blade. This is the head.

Shave about another .5 cm off the body. Roll this a little flatter and make the square eyes and mouth shape. Try to keep the angles really sharp, as the square is a key part of the creeper's appearance.

Place the mouth and eyes on the head and press very, very gently to ensure contact throughout. Bake as per package instructions.

Take out of the oven when hard and set aside to cool.

Step 3: Making the Mold

Ensure you are working in a well-ventilated area and that your clothes are covered by something you do not mind getting latex on. A bin liner with holes cut for your head and arms is the ultimate cheapo DIY option. You will also need to cover your work surface with plastic, NOT paper. An old document wallet—the type that would normally hold a sheet of paper in a ring binder—is great for this.

Now fill your drinking or shot glass half full of water. This will hold your brush in between applications of latex and lengthen its life.

Layer by layer, paint latex onto the masters. This will appear to be running straight off, but it is much better to build up multiple fine layers than to try to wait for one to dry. Keep your brush in the water in between applications.

Depending on various factors such as temperature and how much time you have to devote to this each day, this stage could take between a couple of days and a week. Ideally, allow for a week, and put down one layer of latex each day after work. If you are at home, work at 12 hourly intervals. Ensure there are at least eight layers on both masters.

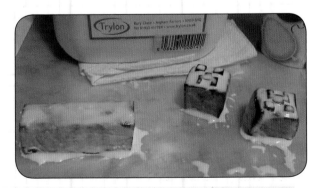

Step 4: First Layer

When the latex mold is finished, carefully peel it back and off the master. You may wish to rub talcum powder down the outside to help prevent it from sticking to itself.

In the deeper recesses of the mouth and eyes, carefully place in half of the black seed beads. You may find that this is fiddly work and that they do not immediately lie flat. If they jump around or move, use a needle or a copper wire to place them back in place.

When they are all lying flat, place a thin layer of the green seed bead mix, just enough to cover the mold base/eyes and mouth.

Cover this with a small layer of resin, mixed as per bottle instructions.

Note: Do not mix the resin in the measuring cup. Pour each fluid into the measuring cup and then wipe thoroughly with kitchen paper until dry before measuring the second fluid. Combine the resin and hardener in the paper cup with a pinched side "spout" and stir it with a chopstick or similar item. To ensure accurate measuring for all future uses of the resin, it is essential the cup is wiped clean of both substances.

When hardened (about 24 hours), fill the molds halfway with beads and then pour resin in. This will sink down amongst the beads, but be cautious with how much you are pouring in—you must keep the balance of resin and beads equal until the molds are filled up to the top.

After another 24 hours, release from the mold and repeat this step for the second creeper.

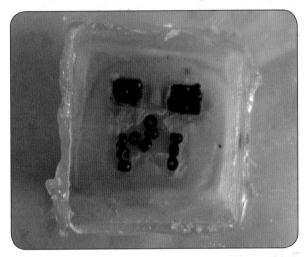

Step 5: Assembling the Creepers

When they came out of the molds, I noticed that the eyes and mouth on my creepers were uniformly black instead of having the "pixelated" effect their bodies did. I'm not sure why this is, but I suspect it is something to do with the quality and type of my black seed beads. If this bothers you, then definitely check the effect with 3–4 of your chosen beads before getting this far in the process.

As you can see however, the individual green beads are visible in the clear resin, giving that fantastic variegated effect that "real" creepers have.

Angle the heads and bodies as you like, making sure they stand up okay, then superglue them together.

Step 6: Dressing the Creepers
For the groom
Make a black top hat out of the black fimo and test it for balance on your groom creeper's head. It is worth leaving making the hat till this point in case you need to make slight allowances for any irregularities in head shape.

Bake it, as per instructions, and leave to cool.

Cut a small length of colored ribbon and wrap around the cooled hat. Glue in place with superglue. Glue hat on head.
For the bride
Cut a tiny piece of gauze in a rough triangle shape. 3 x 3cm would probably be the biggest you'd need; mine is actually less than that.

Arrange with the miniature ribbon rose into a shape and form you like. This will be entirely dependent on your preferences and the shape of your creeper's head, so play around until you have something you like. Glue gauze and rose together.

Place a dot of glue on side of the bride's head and press veil down.

And there you have it: your very own creeper cake toppers.

Glowing Redstone Block

kyluddy
(http://www.instructables.com/id/Minecraft-
Glowing-Redstone-Block/)

This is super easy and uses stuff that you already have! It also makes a great geeky gift!

Step 1: Materials
- Empty tissue box
- Any type of light (as long as you can stuff it into a tissue box)
- Several sheets of thin plastic
- Scissors
- An Xacto knife
- Scotch tape
- Painter's tape
- Red Sharpie
- Ruler
- Pencil
- Gray paint

Step 2: Tissue Box

Once you find an empty tissue box, cut the plastic off around the hole.

Step 3: Covering the Tissue Box in Tape

To paint this tissue box later on, you're going to need to cover it in painters tape first (unless your tissue box is solid gray).

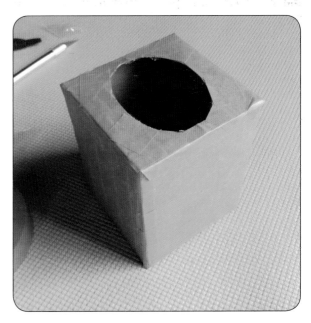

Step 4: Design

Sketch a design (similar to the papercraft pattern above) on all of the sides except for the side with the hole in it, which is the bottom.

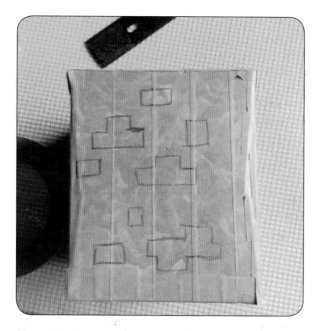

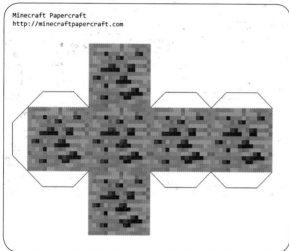

Minecraft Papercraft
http://minecraftpapercraft.com

Step 6: Paint

After you've done this, paint all of the sides (including the bottom) a solid gray color.

Step 5: Cut Out Design

With the Xacto knife, cut out the design you made on all of the sides but the bottom. This part may take a while, and you might have to fiddle with some parts of the box.

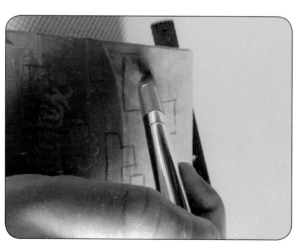

Step 7: Plastic

Cut squares in the piece of plastic that is sized a bit smaller than the sides of the box. Tape each one on the inside of the box so the design has plastic behind it.

Step 8: Color It Red

With the red sharpie, carefully color all of the showing plastic red. (It helps to do small up and down motions.)

Step 9: Light It!

Now, all you have to do is put the light in! My light could fit into the hole sideways and not fall out because it was slightly larger than the hole, but if your light is smaller I would recommend taping it in place or adding another piece of cardboard that the light could go through.

Step 10: Done

Yay!

TNT Clock

Calvin Smith Nutter

(http://www.instructables.com/id/Minecraft-TNT-Clock/)

This is a cool Minecraft-themed cover for a working clock. Not only is it simple to make, but it also looks great when it is finished! It is great for your typical Minecrafter!

Step 1: Supplies

- Small digital clock (with red LED numbers)
- Cardboard box (cube shaped)
   Note: The box must be large enough to contain the clock.
- Lego bricks
- Glue stick
- Utility knife
- Ruler
- Scissors
- A few pieces of paper
- A printer

Step 2: Measuring

Start by measuring the height of the box after the cover has been removed and the box has been turned upside down. Divide that measurement by two to get the midpoint of the box. Then use some spare Lego bricks to construct a stand to raise the clock to the midpoint of the box. The stand you construct should be big enough to raise the clock to the desired height, yet small enough so that the box can still cover it along with the clock. This step will vary quite a lot depending on what type of clock and box are being used in this step. In my case, the face of the clock was tilted, so I had to modify my stand so that the face was not at an angle. To do this, I had the clock rest on the stand at an angle. This unfortunately led to another problem: the clock could easily slide off due to the angle at which it rested. I fixed this problem by establishing a way to prevent the clock from sliding. The main point is: It is important that you construct your stand so that the clock does not slide. Also, be sure that the clock face is flush with the Lego base below. The end result should leave your clock's midpoint at the midpoint of the box.

Note: This stand was built to accommodate my clock. Yours may vary depending on what clock you use.

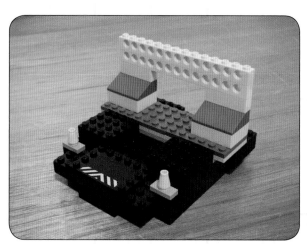

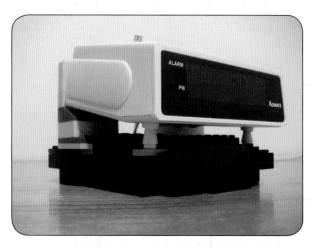

Step 3: Cutting

Now you will need to use your utility knife to cut an opening in the box that corresponds to the face of the clock. To do this cut a small opening in the center of the box to look through in order to see where you need to cut. Slowly cut more and more, making the hole slighter bigger each time, until you have the outline of the clock's face. Any unevenness in the final rectangular cut can be covered up by the paper that will be overlaying the cut. That will be the next step.

Step 4: Designing the Box

Next, you will need to print out a top and sides for the box. There are files on the website that can be printed out, but they may need some adjustments. You will probably need to scale the images down to a size where they will fit on the box nicely. Once you have printed them out at the right size you will then need to cut them out.

Now use your glue stick to cover every side of the box with a thin and sticky coat of glue. Then place the five pieces of paper accordingly. The file name on each image tells you where on the box it needs to be placed. Be sure to print three copies of the one labeled "minecraft_tnt_side". For the one

that goes where the clock should be, simply take the clock and its stand out of the box and place the paper directly over the rectangular hole. Then use your utility knife to cut the part of the paper that is covering the hole.

Step 5: Finishing

Lastly, you will have to make a little cut in the back of the box just big enough for the power cable of the clock to fit through. Plug in your clock, set the time, cover with box, and you're done!

Torch of Protection

woz.artur

(http://www.instructables.com/id/Stick-Coal-the-Minecraft-torch-of-protection/)

I wanted some extra light here, so I decided to build a torch. While looking for the colors, I stumbled upon a model on ThinkGeek. It looks really nice, but my need for light is only on a metaphorical level. I kept it simple: print the model, cut, and glue. Voila!

Step 1: Materials
- Template, printed off on 11" x 17" paper (provided on the website)
- Cutting Board
- Ruler
- Paper Glue
- Knife

Step 2: Print & Cut

Pixels in this model are 1" wide, and the dimensions of the finished torch are 2" x 2" x 10", but you can resize the model before printing.

Print your model on a tabloid-sized paper (11" x 17").

Optional step: Depending on the rigidity of the paper you printed on, you might want to glue the print on a piece of cardboard, something like a cereal box.

Follow instructions and cut slightly inside the printed area.

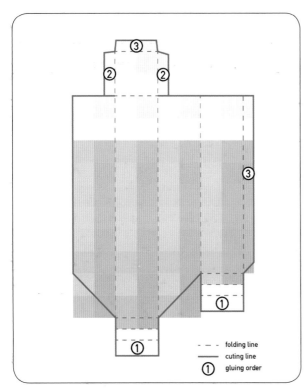

Step 3: Score & Fold!

Flip the model, align the ruler with the folding lines, and score them with the back of the knife's blade. Applying excessive pressure might damage the paper. Fold along all the created grooves—no need to over-bend.

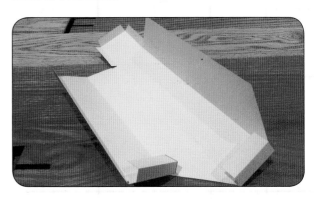

Step 4: Glue!

Apply a thin layer of glue, especially if you're using water-based glue, because the paper will warp.

Gluing areas in the indicated order will ease the assembly.

You don't have to wait until the glue dries between each step, just make sure it holds in place.

Use a pen or a similar tool to apply pressure in the spots that are hard to reach.

Step 5: Throw on a Wall or Offer as a Present

The base is made to fit a piece of a half-inch foamcore (2" x 2 5/16") I had available. You can also use a piece of wood or simply use a tape. Do not hesitate to offer a torch to those who might need one.

Paper Snowflakes

Nicole Smith

(http://www.instructables.com/id/Minecraft-Paper-Snowflakes/)

Minecraft is awesome and so are paper snowflakes. Why not combine them? Enjoy decorating your house this Christmas with these awesome, unique snowflakes!

Step 1: Designing and Supplies

- Files
- Xacto knife
- Small Scissors—small ones are nice so you can get in all the sharp angles
- Paper
- Printer

My snowflakes evolved from my original idea, which was to make a creeper and a sword. I just went for it at first and didn't do any measuring. Then I decided to split up the ideas and do one weapon snowflake and one creeper snowflake. I created squares to signify pixels (1 x 1, 2 x 2, etc.) so I could get the dimensions right. I had to do some messing around with the dimensions so that the creeper wouldn't just be one tall rectangle. I've attached the

Illustrator file if you want At first I had nothing and then I just cut it out and then that was too big of a hole. So later I just added extra pixels.

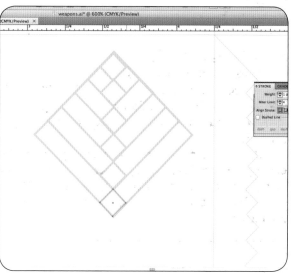

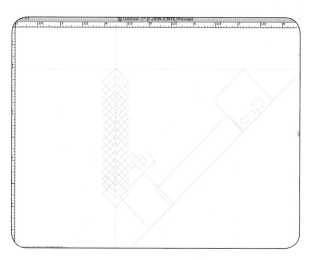

corner with the design to the left opposite corner. Take that corner you just folded over and fold it so the tip meets the top tip, revealing the design again. Flip it over and bring that tip up to the top. Now you have an eight-times-folded snowflake (I hope that made sense!).

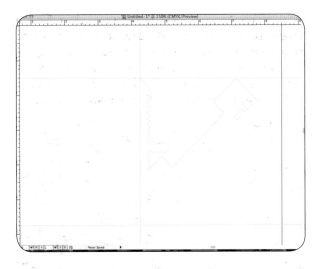

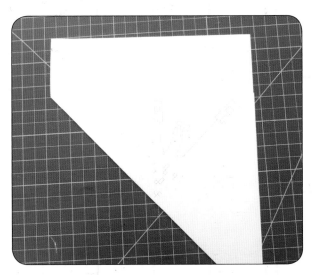

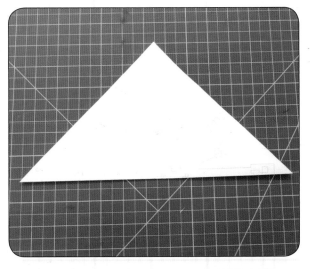

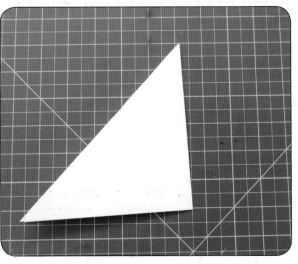

Step 2: Fold

Folding time! If you know what you are doing, go for it. Here is how I folded it to make sure I got good results. First, fold it diagonally so you can cut off the extra paper and you are just left with a square. Don't cut off the design. Now, fold it into a triangle so the design is on the far right and it is facing up. Fold the

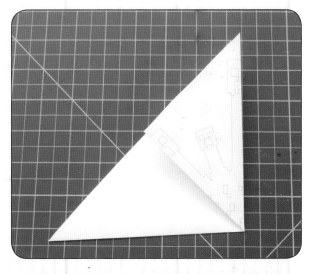

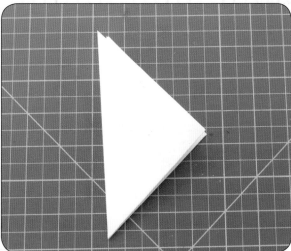

as many pixels as you want. I figured out that for the weapons, it helped to make slits/cuts with an Xacto knife all in one direction down one side of a weapon, and then do the slits going the other way up the other side. It was much easier than trying to cut it like with a scissors. You can see this in images 5 and 6.

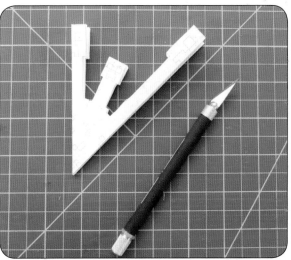

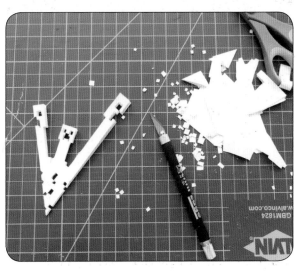

Step 3: Cutting Time!

Cut everything out! For each design, you are cutting out the background, and then for the creepers, you are cutting out their faces. I added little pixels at the bottom of the snowflake so the middle of the snowflake wouldn't be plain. Feel free to add

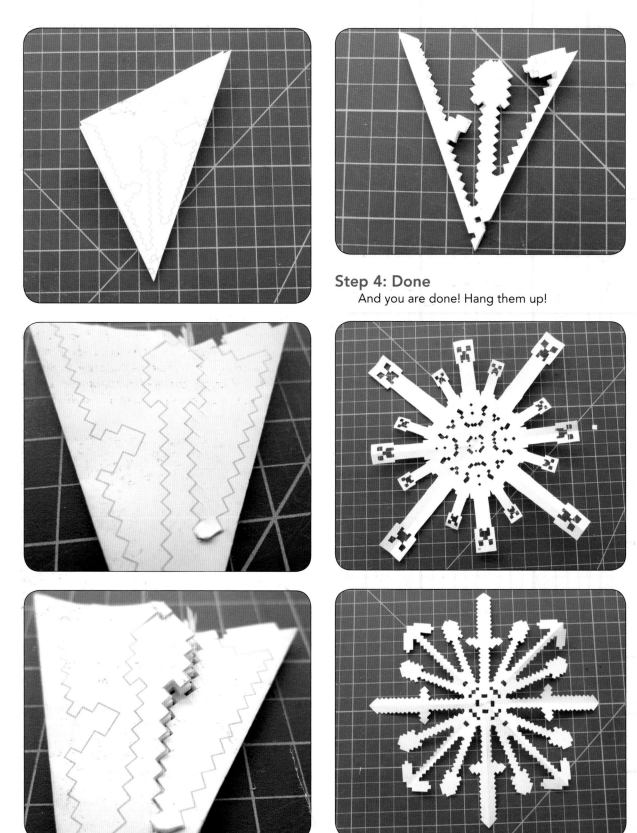

Step 4: Done
And you are done! Hang them up!

Golden Apple Quilt Block

sylrig
(http://www.instructables.com/id/Making-a-Minecraft-Golden-Apple-Block/)

In Minecraft, the Golden Apple is a rare object that can restore all health. With that as an analogy, a Golden Apple quilt block can be used to create a pillow covering (shown here) or a quilt for someone who is ailing.

Step 1: Tools and Materials

- An enlarged printout of the Golden Apple Fabric for the apple (if you don't have it in scrap, buy the minimum cut you can—often a quarter yard. You can also use precut fat quarters.)
- Fabric for the pillow case (1 1/2 yards for this 20" x 20" covering)
- Scissors
- A sewing machine

Step 2: Diagramming the Block

This is how I diagrammed the block. You may find a way that makes more sense to you, but basically, you will need to break it down into rows.

In this diagram, I have six rows. Each unit is 1/2" square. To add seam allowances of 1/4" on each side, 1/2" is added to the total measurement. Thus, a 4-unit piece would measure 1" square on the block but be cut at 1 1/2" square to include seam allowances.

One thing to note: The white "reflection" in the center of the apple is not necessarily the same as the background color, also white on paper, which surrounds the apple. In my case, I found a mottled green that looked a little like the Minecraft grass. Thus, all the pieces surrounding the apple would be cut in green.

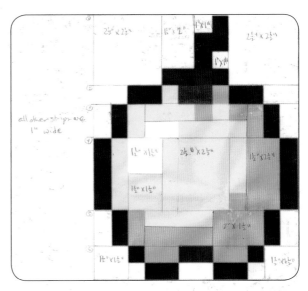

Step 3: Sew Row by Row

Here is an example of how row 4 is cut and pieced. First, the pieces are cut out and laid according to the block diagram. Any pieces that are in two parts (such as the white top and golden bottom piece third from left) will be sewn together, and then the strip is pieced.

Step 4: Complete the Apple

When you have completed all six rows, sew them together to piece the apple. The block should measure 6 1/2" x 8".

Step 5: Add Borders

If you are making a block to include in a quilt, you can simply add 1" x 8" borders of background fabric to each side and a single 1" x 8 1/2" border to the top, and you will have an 8 1/2" block.

If you are making a 20" x 20" pillow covering, add 7 1/2" x 8" borders to the side, then 20 1/2" x 6 1/2" borders to the top and bottom to create a 20 1/2" square. You can also make it a little bigger and allow for 1/2" seam allowances from here on, as I did.

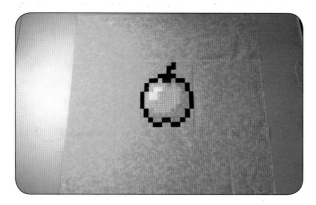

Step 6: Quilt the Outline

Cut a piece of white muslin to the size of your finished top (in this case, 20 1/2" square). Pin wrong sides together and machine quilt around the outline of the apple. I quilted both sides of the black outline; you could quilt within the apple for extra stability.

Step 7: Complete the Pillow Covering

Cut and hem a piece of your background fabric approximately 20 1/2" x 6" (hemmed measurement) and lay it on top of the pillow top with the hem down, right sides together.

Cut and hem another piece of background fabric approximately 20 1/2" x 16" (hemmed measurement) and lay it on top of that, right side down.

Now simply pin and sew all the way around. When you turn it right side out, you will have a pillow covering with an envelope opening.

Creeper Pillow Cushion

Lizzy Taylor

(http://www.instructables.com/id/Minecraft-creeper-pillow-cushion/)

Both my sons enjoy playing Minecraft, so I decided to make them each a quilted Minecraft Creeper Cushion. As the game uses a very pixelated format, the objects lend themselves to being pieced out of smaller squares of fabric. I started with a screen shot that showed the face of a creeper very clearly and chose to use 2" finished squares, giving a finished face size of 16" and an overall cushion size of 22" square.

This Instructable shows how to make a cushion cover using a no-zip method by skipping the piecing and quilting; the method could be used for any fabric. The addition of borders and how to measure for them is also included. After following this Instructable a reader should be able to make a plain or simple pieced cushion cover. These are ideal as gifts and also great when you cannot find a store-bought throw pillow or cushion to match your decor.

Step 1: Requirements

- 44 mixed mid- to light-green and grey 2 1/2" squares of fabric
- 8 black 2 1/2" squares of fabric
- 12 dark green 2 1/2" squares of fabric
- Black fabric for border
- Green fabric for binding
- 24" (60cm x 60cm) square of quilt batting/wadding
- 24" (60cm x 60cm) square of muslin (or ugly fabric or leftover fabric, but quilting weight or lighter to minimize bulk)
- 22" (56cm) pillow form/cushion pad
- Scissors
- Iron
- Ironing board
- Sewing thread
- Sewing machine
- Rotary cutter, mat, and ruler (not essential, but these tools make cutting accurate strips and squares much easier and faster)

Step 2: Sew the Cushion Front

Lay out your fabric squares to make the face of the creeper. I used the very dark green squares as part of the eyes and mouth rather than using all black. If you have a digital camera take a picture of your layout to help you keep the squares in your chosen pattern as you sew them together.

Sew the squares into rows using a 1/4" seam and press the seams on each row in opposite directions (e.g., row 1 to the right, row 2 to the left, etc.). Sew the rows together to make the creeper face, which should end up at 16 1/2" square. Press all the long seams carefully, ensuring you don't end up with fabric tucks at the fold.

Measure across the center of your creeper's face (should be 16 1/2", but mine was 16 3/8") and cut two strips of black fabric this long by 3 1/2" wide. Sew these to the top and bottom of the face and press the seam towards the border. Now measure across the "height" of your face (should be 22 1/2"), including the borders, and cut two strips of black fabric this long by 3 1/2" wide. Sew these to the sides of the face and again press the seam towards the border. If your borders are longer than the central measurement across your center they will end up being wavy. This would not be a big problem on a small project like this, but on a larger quilt or a wall hanging it would be quite noticeable.

Step 3: Quilt the Cushion Front

Iron your 24" square of muslin (or other fabric) and lay it down on a firm surface, smoothing out any wrinkles. Lay your batting on top of it and, finally, place your creeper face centrally on top of the batting with the right side uppermost.

Pin your layers securely together so that the layers do not shift while you quilt them.

If you have a walking foot for your sewing machine, fit it now and choose a suitable thread for your quilting. First, I used black thread and quilted "in the ditch" around the eyes and mouth and around the border. Then I changed to my darning foot, dropped the feed dogs, and did a square spiral in the eyes and the mouth of the creeper. Finally, keeping the darning foot fitted, I changed to the variegated green thread, then meander-quilted across the mid- and light-green areas and did a square meander in the black borders.

After quilting, trim your batting and muslin backing so the edges are even with the edges of the cushion front.

Step 4: Make the Cushion Back

Measure your cushion front; it should be about 22 1/2" square, but may have contracted a bit with the quilting—mine measured up at 22". You now need two pieces of fabric for the cushion back. The length of each will be the length of the front, and the width will be 2/3 of the width, so in this case 15".

On the wrong side of the fabric draw a line 1" in from one long edge on each piece. Fold the fabric to the line and press along the fold, then fold over again at the line and press again to enclose the raw edge. Sew along the fold to secure the fabric in a 1/4" hem. Repeat for the other piece of cushion-back fabric. I chose to use the green thread for this because it looked more attractive and was easier to see for the photos.

Lay the cushion front right side down and then place the two cushion back pieces so that the hemmed edges overlap each other and the raw edges of the back fabric match the raw edges of the cushion front. Sew all around the raw edges as close to the edge as you can. This line of stitching will be hidden by the binding, so I again used a contrasting color to make the pictures clearer.

Step 5: Bind the Cushion Cover

Measure all around the outside of the cushion—the perimeter should measure about 90". You need to prepare a length of binding this long, plus an extra 5" for each corner, i.e., about 110"!

Cut three 2 1/2" strips across the width of your binding fabric and sew them together on the diagonal as shown, then trim off the excess fabric and press in half lengthwise with the raw edges matching. Apply the binding.

Once you have applied the binding you can slip your pillow form/cushion into the cover and lean against your creeper!

Minecraft Toys

Knit Creeper

Enderman Plushie

Wither Plushie

Stuffed Creeper Doll

Pig USB Holder

Knit Creeper
Toadash
(http://www.instructables.com/id/Knitted-Minecraft-Creeper/)

I like to play Minecraft. I also like to knit, so I decided to make myself a plush creeper. I was pretty sure it would be easy because a creeper is just made up of boxes.

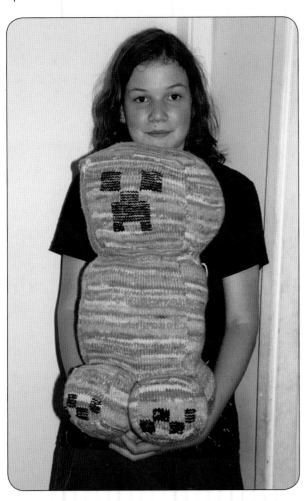

Step 1: Materials
- Yarn—I used 8 ply acrylic yarn. My mom found some really cool multi-colored green that was perfect. I used about 2 1/2 100g balls.
- Black yarn—for the face markings and the toes
- Knitting needles—I used 3.75mm
- Stuffing—I don't know how much I used because it wasn't a new bag

Step 2: The Body Pieces

All the pieces are just squares or rectangles made doing stocking stitch.

Head: Make 6 pieces that are 40 stitches wide by 42 rows.

Body: Make two pieces 40 stitches wide by 21 rows—these are the top and bottom pieces of the body. Next make two pieces that are 40 stitches wide by 63 rows—these are the front and back pieces of the body. Finally make two pieces 20 stitches wide by 63 rows—these are the sides of the body.

Feet: Make four feet. Each foot is made with six pieces that are 20 stitches wide by 21 rows (24 pieces in total).

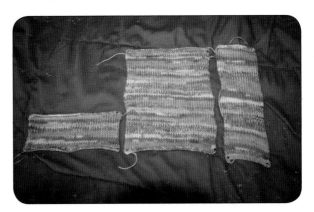

101

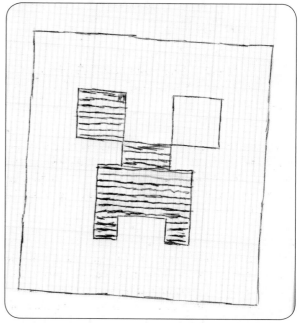

Step 3: Sewing It Up

Sew up the pieces for the head and feet into cubes, then stuff and sew up the opening. Sew the body pieces so that the long narrow pieces are the sides and the wider long pieces are the front and back. Stuff and sew up the opening.

Before you sew the pieces together, you have to put the face and the toes on. These are stitched on using black yarn. The toes are just four squares in a checkerboard pattern across the bottom of the foot. There is a picture on graph paper to show how to do the face.

When the markings are sewn on, you can put the creeper together. The feet get sewn on the bottom of the body—two in front and two behind. Then the head is attached on top of the body.

Enderman Plushie

MasamuneX

(http://www.instructables.com/id/Make-an-Enderman-Plushie-from-Minecraft/)

In this Instructable I'm going to try to teach you how to create your very own Enderman plushie. You will also be able to apply these same techniques to create other Minecraft creatures and, quite possibly, unforgettable holiday moments.

Step 1: Materials and Tools

Here is a list of the materials that I used. Surely you can substitute these for other brands, quantities, and types of materials. Materials List:

- 1 yard Sew Classic Velour Black (or your choice of black color fabric)
- Coats & Clark Dual Duty XP General Purpose Thread – 250yds (1 black, 1 red, 1 light pink thread to match the pink ribbon color)
- 1 yard pink ribbon 1 x 1/2" width
- 1 yard fuchsia ribbon 1 x 1/2" width
- Poly-fil Fiber 32 oz
- Sharpie Metallic Fine Point Markers–Silver

Basic Tools List:
- Sewing needles
- Sewing pins
- Ruler/straight edge/yardstick
- Scissors
- Masking tape
- Seam ripper

Step 2: Understanding the Fabric Flow and Layout

The first step to making this Enderman is to consider how all of your dimensions are to be drawn onto the material. If you are using the material I suggested then this step is of great importance. The velour fabric has somewhat of a pattern to it. If you slide your hand across the material in a back and forth motion it will have different colors and characteristics. One way feels smooth and lighter in color while the other way appears darker and seems to have a sense of resistance.

You want to draw your dimensions on the material so that it flows in a single direction. You want all your pieces to flow from the smooth side downward from head to toe. If you are not careful during this process the final product may end up appearing inconsistent.

Now that we understand our pattern layout we can proceed to applying it to the back of our material.

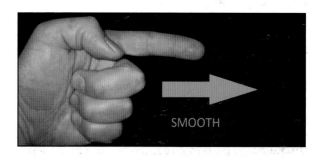

SMOOTH

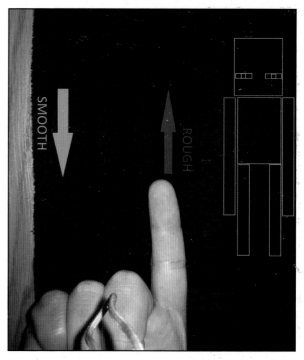

SMOOTH

ROUGH

SMOOTH

Step 3: Understanding the Dimensions and Applying Them!

The measurements of the Enderman plushie were derived from its in-game pixel dimensions divided by two.

Listed below are the pixel dimensions of the Enderman followed by how many pieces you will need at said dimensions.

Naturally, as with any sewing project, you are going to leave some extra material on the outside of your work piece. You will need to do this for all 35 pieces. So for example the first measurement below is 4" (H) x 4" (W). Your actual dimensions are going to be 5" (H) x 5" (W). This leaves 1/2" of space on all sides. Savvy?

Head:	Pixels	Inches
Height:	8	4"
Width:	8	4"
Side:	8	4"

6 pieces at 4" (H) x 4" (W)

Body:	Pixels	Inches
Height:	10	5"
Width:	8	4"
Side:	4	2"

Front and Back: 2 pieces 5" (H) x 4" (W)
Sides: 2 pieces 5" (H) x 2" (W)
Bottom: 1 piece 2" (H) x 4" (W)

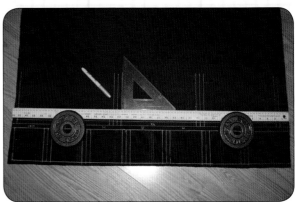

Arms:	Pixels	Inches
Height:	25	12 1/2"
Width:	2	1"
Side:	2	1"

8 pieces at 12 1/2" (H) x 1" (W)

Legs:	Pixels	Inches
Height:	19	9.5"
Width:	2	1"
Side:	2	1"

8 pieces at 9.5" (H) x 4" (W)

Tops/Bottoms of Arms and Legs (T&B's)

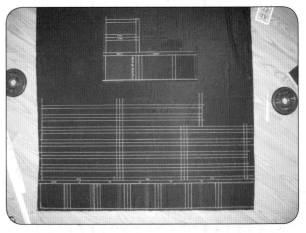

T/B L&A	Pixels	Inches
Height:	1	1"
Width:	1	1"

8 pieces at 1"(H) x 1" (W)

Applying those dimensions.

Now take out your metallic Sharpie and yard stick (triangle is optional). It also helps to have some weights (or random heavy items) to hold down the fabric and yard stick while you are marking the material. That way you can concentrate on creating the straightest line possible without anything moving around. In addition, do not press down too hard while you are moving your marker across the material as this may cause the fabric to stretch and ruin the alignment. Instead try to simply glide it over the material.

I strongly urge you to draw an arrow pointing in the direction in which the pattern flows. This will come in handy later when you begin stitching all the pieces together.

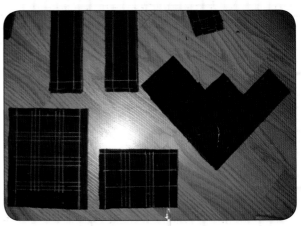

This whole process is tedious and time consuming. Take your time and pay attention to the spacing between each piece.

Step 4: Cutting Out the Pattern and Crafting Ender Eyes

Phew! I told you that would take a while.

Now you can begin cutting the pattern out.

1. Start off by cutting out the pieces into large manageable chunks. Head, Body, Legs, Arms, T&B's.
2. Next, start cutting out the individual pieces, making sure to NOT cut off the extra 1/2" space between pieces.
3. Organize all of your pieces. Try to keep all the pieces with the arrows facing one direction. You should have 35 pieces total.
4. Place these pieces somewhere safe until later.

Crafting Ender eyes.

In this step we are going to need these dimensions and materials for the eyes of an Enderman.

Outer eye:	Pixels	Inches
Height:	1	1/2"
Width:	3	1 1/2"
Between them:	2	1"
From bottom of face:	3	1 1/2"
2 pieces at 1/2" (H) x 1 1/2" (W)		
Pupils:	Pixels	Inches
Height:	1	1/2"
Width:	1	1/2"
2 pieces at 1/2" (H) x 1 1/2" (W)		

Crafting the outer eye
Materials:
- 1 1/2" Light pink ribbon
- Light pink thread

Since the light pink ribbon is already the perfect width, all we need to do is create 1/2" of height. Start by folding about 1/8" to 1/4" of the upper edge of the ribbon downward. Try to evenly align the left and right sides of the ribbon as much as possible. Once you have done so, run the back of your fingernail or another hard object over the ribbon a few times to try to create a crease. Now use a sewing machine or hand sew the top edge of the ribbon. After you have sewn the top edge fold the ribbon over again and use a ruler to measure exactly 1/2". Use the same technique to complete the outer portion of the eye, then cut it away from the rest of the ribbon. Repeat these steps until you have two outer eyes. When finishing be sure to pull the thread into the back of the outer eye and knot it to keep the thread secure as well as to give it a cleaner look.

Crafting the pupil
Materials:
- 1 1/2" magenta/fuchsia ribbon
- Red thread

You will use the 1 1/2" magenta/fuchsia ribbon with red thread and the same techniques explained above to create two pupils for the Enderman eyes.

Uniting the eyes

Take the one pupil part and place it on top of an outer eye part. Use them to create a plus-like symbol.

Try to center them as much as possible, using a ruler if necessary. Now fold the pupil downward and around to the bottom of the outer eye. Using your preferred sewing method and red thread, sew around the edges of the pupil to secure it to the outer eye to form a complete Enderman eye. Again, make sure to bring the thread to the back of the eye and knot it on the back side. Trim any excess. Use the same technique to complete the second eye.

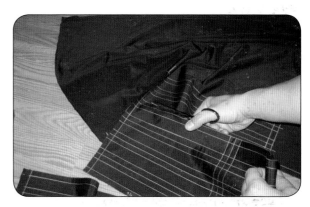

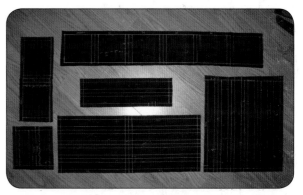

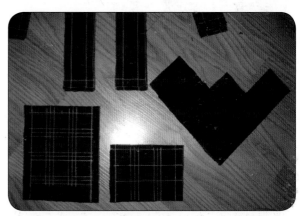

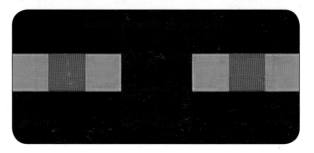

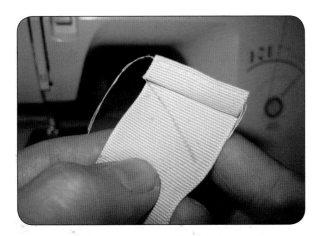

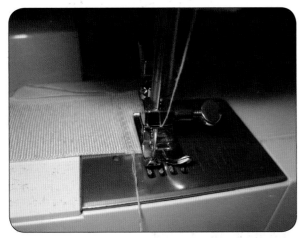

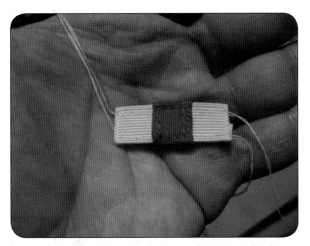

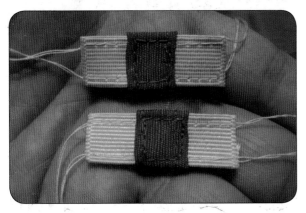

Step 5: Attaching the Eyes, Creating a Perfect Fit

Masking the area around the face

In this step you are going to need three sewing pins, masking tape, and a ruler to attach the eyes of the Enderman.

First grab one of the six 4" x 4" face pieces you cut out earlier and flip it over so you are looking at the back of the fabric. Starting on one side of the square, push your pins through the line—one in each corner and one in the middle.

Flip the fabric over, with the pins closest to you. Place the ruler on the back side of the pins to make them stand upright. Now that they are all standing straight grab a piece of masking tape, and, holding it tautly, place the tape as close as possible to the three pins. This should give you a straight and true line.

Repeat on all sides until you have masking tape around the edges of your work piece.

Straight line for the eyes

Once again the issue about pattern flow arises. Ensure that the smooth direction of the fabric faces downward or towards you. Flip the fabric so you're looking on the back side with the arrow still pointing towards you, then measure 1 1/2" up from the bottom line and make a mark. Do this on both left and right sides so you can achieve a straight and true line. Just as before, you are going to push the three sewing pins through the line you just drew, one in each corner and one in the middle. Flip the fabric to the front side of the material and use the ruler to prop up the pins, tautly stretching a piece of masking tape across the front, giving you a straight line. Remove the pins.

Attaching the eyes

Finally, you are able to set the eyes into place. Keeping them as straight as possible, sew them onto the fabric using your preferred sewing method with matching light pink thread. Sew a box pattern only around the visible light pink/outer eye area. Avoid sewing into the pupil as the colors will not match. Move the thread to the back side of the fabric and knot it to secure the thread.

With the eyes in place you are free to remove the masking tape, as it is no longer serves a purpose.

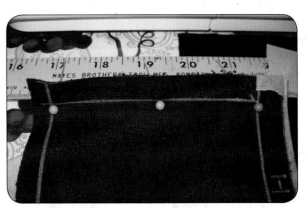

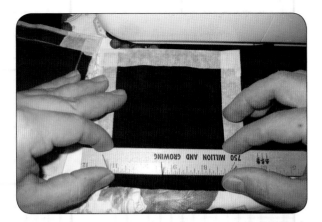

Step 6: You Reap What You Sew!

Now the fun begins. All the pieces you are going to sew are six-sided squares or rectangles. Basically the goal is to create a box with the nice side of the fabric facing the inside and the pattern flowing in a single direction. The process is simple and redundant, yet arduous. You apply this same sewing method to all the parts with a few exceptions.

Sewing the arms and legs

Take all the arm/leg pieces and pin and sew them according to the diagram or whichever method you prefer to achieve a hollow box.

Sewing the head

Take four of six pieces, pin them, and sew them according to the diagram or whichever method you prefer to achieve a hollow box.

Sewing the body

Using both of the 5" x 4" pieces and both 5" x 2" pieces, pin and sew them according to the diagram or whichever method you prefer to achieve a hollow box.

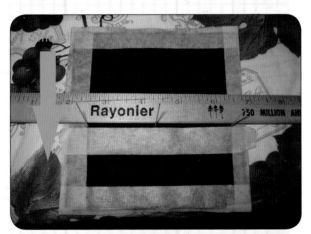

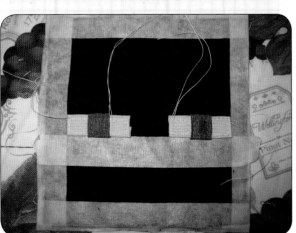

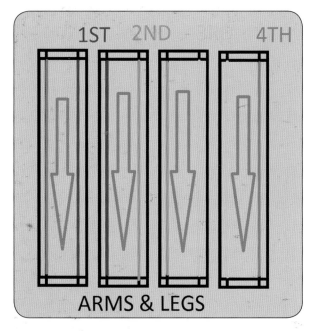

ARMS & LEGS

1ST 2ND 4TH

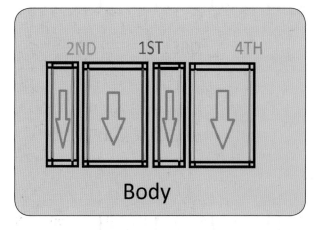

Body

2ND 1ST 4TH

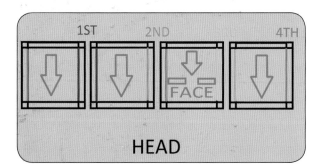

HEAD

1ST 2ND FACE 4TH

Step 7: Tops and Bottoms

Remember the 1" x 1" squares? Well, now you have the pleasure of sewing them to the tops and bottoms of each arm and leg. Considering the limited amount of space, I would suggest sewing these on by hand. The bottom of the arm/leg, which is also the bottom of the smooth side, is going to be sewed all the way around the 1" x 1" section. The top of the arm/leg is only going to be sewed around half of the 1" x 1". The green color in the diagram represents what will be sewed during this stage.

Trimming and cleaning the edges of the arms and legs

Once you finish with all eight, you're going to trim about half the length of material off the edges of the arms and legs. After you have trimmed off the excess edges, the material will need to be shaken/ cleaned off, as it will be shedding lots of material. I would recommend doing this outside or over a carpet where it can easily be vacuumed up, because things will get very messy.

Fiber filling the arms and legs

Next, take the arms/legs and turn them inside out. They are ready to be stuffed with FiberFill. Generously fill them with FiberFill and use something such as a ruler to help push it down to the bottom. The FiberFill will have a tendency to lump up. If this occurs, place the affected area between the palms of your hands and roll it back and forth as if you were trying to warm up your hands.

Next we will move onto closing the seams of the arms and legs.

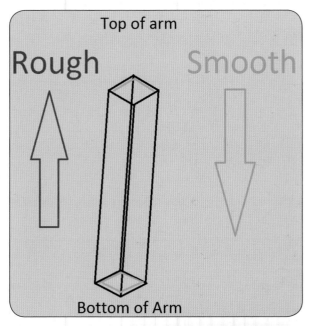

Top of arm

Rough   Smooth

Bottom of Arm

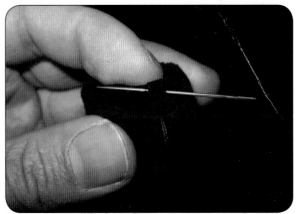

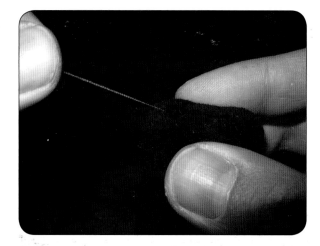

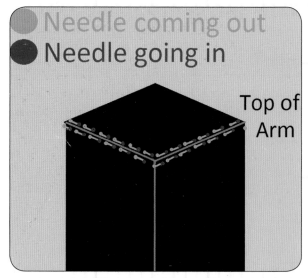

Needle coming out
Needle going in

Top of Arm

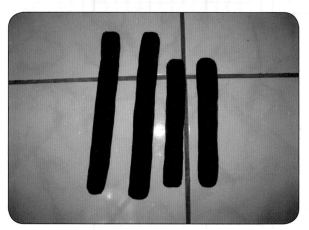

Step 8: Closing the Seams of the Arms and Legs

When you feel that a decent amount of material has been placed inside each appendage you're going to fold the fabric inward on the top and bottom lips. You want to make this as even as possible. Now we can start the slip stitch. Take your black thread and thread it onto a sewing needle. Knot your thread a few times and place your needle on the inside of the lower rightmost point of the opening. Push it from the inside and pull it out to the outside. Then you will want to pierce the needle through the upper lip and maneuver the needle back out of the upper lip just slightly away from where you entered. Alternate this up and down until you get to the very end of the seam. Look at the diagram to see how to perform a slip stitch.

Here you want to hold the appendage in one hand while pulling the thread and needle with the other. Doing this will pull the lips together and seal the hole. Now you are free to knot the thread in whatever manner you feel suits you best. I personally just try to find the last stitch I made and knot it to that.

Only three more appendages to go.

Step 9: Finishing the Head and Body
Finishing the head

Now that the appendages are all finished you can focus on finishing up the head and body.

Start by taking the last two pieces that belong to the head. These pieces will obviously need to be attached to the top and bottom of the head to complete the box. I personally preferred to have the smooth side of the pattern flowing backwards to the back of the head. Stitch the last two pieces in place.

Now you have a head that is stitched together inside out. Do not be alarmed—it was done this way for a reason. Using scissors or a seam ripper, cut a hole along the bottom of the head. The bottom of the head is the side where the eyes are the closest. Use the attached picture get a idea of how long your cut should be.

Now you have an Enderman head that is ready to be stuffed. Fill the head with FiberFill generously. When you feel that enough material is filled you have to use the slip stitch to close the seam. Achievement complete! You finished the head. Set it aside.
Finishing the body

Next take the last piece that belongs to the body, which is a 4" x 2" piece. Pin it to the bottom of the body. The bottom of the body is the bottom of the smooth side. The pattern flow of the bottom piece does not matter much because it's on the bottom side of the plushie. However, I personally wanted the smooth side to flow from the front of the plushie towards the back. Once you have it in place, stitch it. Now the body is complete and now we can move on to preparing the body for the reception of the head.

Masking the body

Remember the trick with the three sewing pins? It's time to bring those items back out. This time we are going to implement this technique on the open end of the body. Work this magic all the way around until you have a masking tape ring 1/2" down from the top of the open end of the body.

Now fold the material inward towards the inside of the body. You are going to fold it in until the top of the open end just barely shows the material. Next you are going to attach the head to the body.

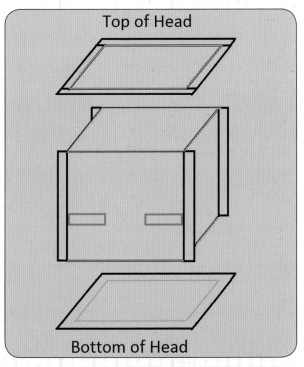

Top of Head

Bottom of Head

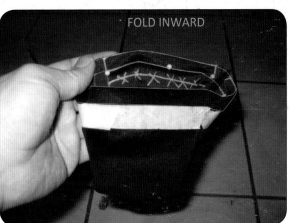

FOLD INWARD

Step 10: Uniting the Head and Body

Finally it is all starting to come together. In this step you will need a couple of pins to hold the body along the bottom of the head.

Now take the Enderman's body and try to align it up against the head's profile. Pin one side first and then pin the opposite side. Start the slip stitch on the left side of the Enderman's face and work your way around to the right side. You are not going to sew the back of neck shut as this will serve as a way for you to fill the body with fiber. Also you may have to use more than one seam to complete this step. I like to pull the stitch tight about every 1 1/2" to 2".

Filler up!

Once you have completed the unification, begin to fill the body with fiber. When you feel that there

is enough material on the inside of the body use a slip stitch to close the back of the neck. You can now remove the masking tape off of the body as it has served its purpose.

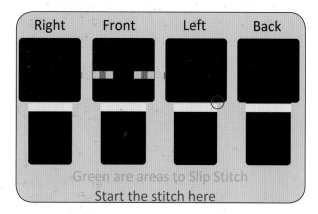

Right   Front   Left   Back

Green are areas to Slip Stitch
Start the stitch here

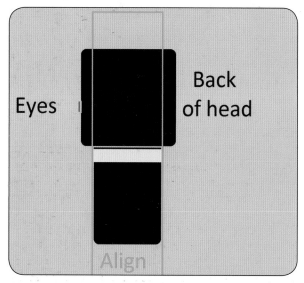

Eyes   Back of head

Align

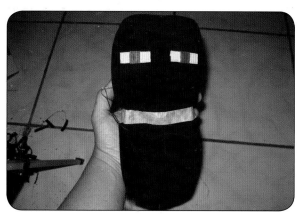

Step 11: Attaching the Limbs.

You are in the home stitch! All you have left to do is to attach the limbs. Once again you are going to ye ole slip stitch to attach all of the limbs to the body.

The legs

The legs are going to be attached to the bottom on the outermost sides, aligning them directly center of the side profile. You will need to stitch these all the way around the very top of the legs. If you prefer you could stitch them only on the front, giving them a hinging effect; however, I stitched them all the way around. Once you are done it's time to attach the arms.

The arms

The arms are only going to be stitched along the upper innermost point of the arm. Basically right where an arm pit would be. Stitch both arms in place and then move on to the final step.

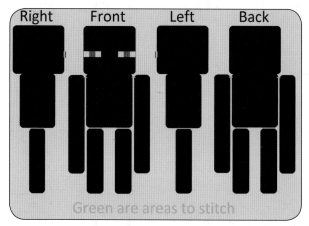

Right   Front   Left   Back

Green are areas to stitch

Step 11: Next Step?

Hold your Enderman up in the air and wait for the treasure chest theme from Zelda to play!

DUN DUN DUN DUHHHHHHHHHHHHHHHHH-HHHH!!!

Now all you have to do is try to keep him (or her) away from dark-colored cola (they love the stuff) and presents, and never, under any circumstances, look them in the eyes!

Wither Plushie

MasamuneX

(http://www.instructables.com/id/Make-a-
Wither-Plushie-from-Minecraft/)

Is this lucky little birthday boy/Minecraft freak holding the world's first Wither Plushie? Although highly improbable, it's possible. Want to know what else is possible? The ability to create one of your very own! In this Instructable I will help you craft a Wither for yourself, a friend, or anyone else who was lucky enough to have made your acquaintance.

Step 1: Tools & Materials

- Sewing machine
- Sewing needles
- Scissors
- Seam ripper
- Ruler or
- Yard stick or t-square
- Right angle ruler (optional)
- Push pins
- Masking tape
- Clear tape

Below are the materials that I used to create my Wither. You may substitute these materials for others, but keep in mind that the fabric will reflect the overall quality of the final product. I purchased all of my materials from Joann's. If you're doing the same then check their website for coupons before you go or download their app to get the coupons. Another thing to consider is that if you have a competing store nearby you may be able to price match items and coupons.

Materials:

Fabric—1 yard of Costume Suede Caviar Solid Alova ($8.99)

Ribbon—1 yard of 1 1/2" wide ribbon ($1.49)

Thread—100M thread (color "flint") ($1.80)
Thread—250 yards (color "black") ($2.99)
Stuffing—FiberFill Stuffing 32oz ($8.99)
Marker—Sharpie, Metallic Silver ($4.99)

If your store doesn't have the Caviar Solid Alova you can also use Sew Classic Suedecloth-Caviar Solid Microsuede or Costume Suedecloth–Black Fringe Alova.

Step 1: The Dimensions

So before we embark on our journey, we need to first decide how big we want our Wither to be. In my previous Minecraft plushie projects, the dimensions were derived by counting each pixel or block on a mob and converting it to an inch. This methodology would have ended up making a Wither that is 27" high by 24" wide. Personally, I had difficulties trying to fit all these dimensions within the one yard of fabric. So I decided to decrease the Wither's size by 25 percent, which resulted in a mob that spanned 20 1/4" high by 18" wide. The dimensions below are the in-game block dimensions. If you decide to reduce the size of your Wither as I have, then you will have to multiply each dimension below by the percentage of decrease. So, for example, if you wanted to make a Wither that was 20 percent smaller than the block dimensions, then the equation for the main head would be 8 x .20 = 1.60; 8 – 1.60 = 6.4. So 6.4" = 6 6/16" or 6 3/8". For those who wish to craft a Wither at 75 percent of its full size, I have added a picture that has the dimensions as well as the number of pieces that need to be created for each part.

Note: Naturally, as with any sewing project, you are going to leave some extra material on the outside of your work piece. You will need to do this for all of your pieces. So, for example, if your first measurement is 6" (L) x 6" (W), your actual dimensions are going to be 7" (H) x 7" (W), leaving 1/2" of space on all sides. Verstehen?

Dimensions of in-game blocks (Length x Width x Height):

Main Head:

Length 8   Width 8   Height 8

Sub-Head (shouldered heads):

Length 6   Width 6   Height 6

Torso: Length 3   Width 3   Height 16

Ribs: Length 4   Width 4   Height 4

Shoulder   Easy   (easier but not to true dimensions):

Length 20 Width 3   Height 3

Shoulder Harder (truer dimensions):

Length Top 16   Length Middle 16

Length Bottom 20   Width 3   Height 3

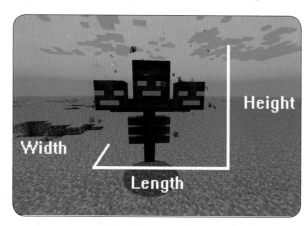

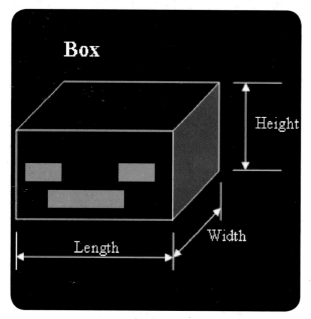

75% of Block dimension and # of pieces

.25 = 1/4"
.50 or .5 = 1/2"
.75 = 3/4"

Main Head
6 pieces at 6" x 6"

Sub Head
12 pieces at 4.5" x 4.5"

Torso
4 pieces at 12" x 2.25

Ribs
24 pieces at 3" x 1.5"

Shoulder (Easy)
4 pieces at 15" x 2.25"

Shoulder (harder) view the picture diagram
● 1 piece at 9"
● 1 piece at 15"
● 2 pieces at (side panels)
● 2 pieces at .75"
● 2 pieces at 3"
● 2 pieces at 1.5"

End Pieces

Torso Ends
2 pieces at 2.25" x 2.25"

Shoulder Ends
2 pieces at 2.25" x 2.25"

Rib Ends
12 pieces at 1.5" x 1.5"

Face

Eyes
6 pieces at 1.5" x .75"

Mouth
3 pieces at 3" x .75

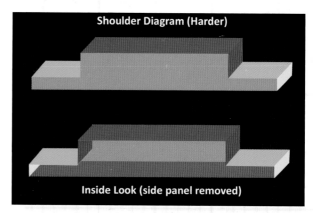

Shoulder Diagram (Harder)

Inside Look (side panel removed)

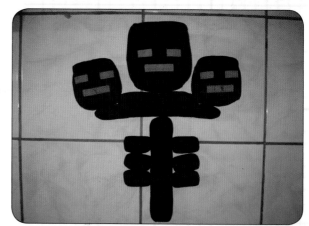

Step 2: Patience Is a Virtue

In this step you will be faced with the tedious task of sketching the dimensions on the back of your material using your metallic Sharpie. Feel free to use some heavy cans or weights to help keep the fabric from sliding around. If you find that you are crawling on top of the material just to draw your patterns, don't be afraid to cut it in half to make it more manageable. Also don't forget to leave at least 1/2" of space around the perimeter of each piece!

This process is laborious and will test your patience. So be sure to take your time and maybe listen to some of your favorite tunes while you slave away. Once completed, divide the pattern into chunks, grouping them with like pieces for easy identification. Be mindful of your work area as the Sharpie may bleed through the fabric and leave freckles all over.

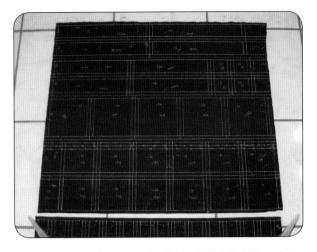

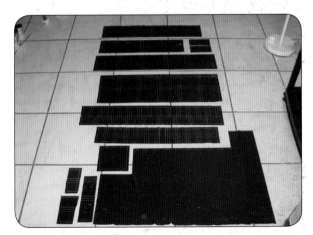

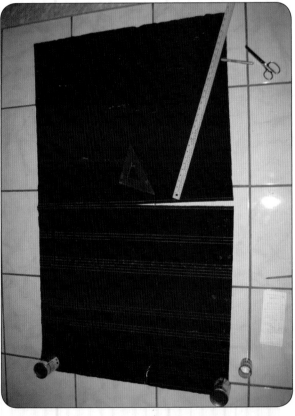

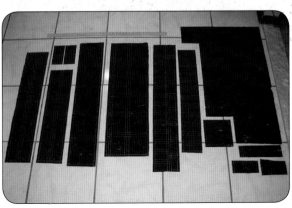

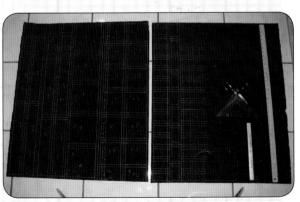

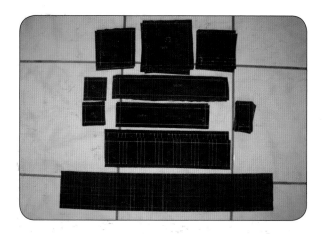

Step 3: Worse than Cerberus

In this step you are going to start sewing the heads of the Wither. There are three heads that need to be crafted in this process. Basically, you're going to sewing them in the shape of a crucifix. (Keep back, you ghoulish Nether fiends!) Check out the diagram to help show you the order in which it should be sewn. Once you complete all three, move on to the next step.

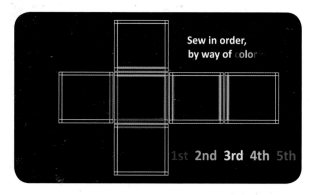

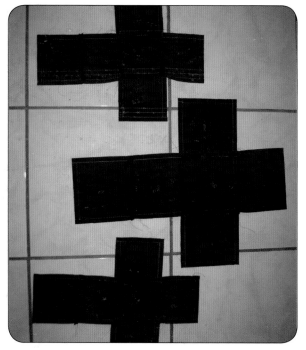

Step 4: What Big Eyes . . . and Teeth You Have, Grandma!

In this step you're going to be crafting the eyes and mouth of the Wither. Each head has the same eye and mouth dimensions, so you are going to create three sets. These sets consist of six eyes and three mouths. The instructions below were written with 75 percent dimensions in mind. If you are using a different ratio then adjust your values accordingly.

The Eyes

Go grab your 1 1/2" ribbon and fold it over about 3/8th of an inch. Make it as even as possible on both sides, then pinch the folded end. With the ribbon clamped between your index finger and your thumb, rake your nail across it a few times. This will help set a nice crease in place. Being careful to keep the ribbon as straight as possible, place it in your sewing machine and run a stitch across.

Now, measure from the newly sewn end of the ribbon and make a mark 3/4" down. Once marked, fold the lipped side of the ribbon in on itself. Make a nice creased line then place it in your sewing machine and run a stitch across. Cut the newly sewn eye from the rest of the ribbon and use a needle to pull any remaining thread from the front of the eye to the rear. Knot the ends and leave a few inches of thread so that you may pull the thread under the flaps on the back side of the eye.

The Mouth

Take your ribbon and measure a length of 3 3/4" and cut it off. Hold the ribbon vertically and fold both outer edges in towards one another until they meet. Press both sides down firmly between your thumb and index finger, creating a crease. Once you have a decent crease formed, use a few pieces of clear tape to help hold the work piece together. Try to make the piece as symmetrical as possible. When you feel you have achieved a symmetrical piece, carefully place it in your sewing matching and stitch it along the two longest sides close to the edges.

Now take the two 3/4" ends and fold them back onto the rear side of the mouth piece. Adjust the amount of material that is being tucked behind until you achieve 3". Once adjusted properly, stitch both sides. When you have completed all nine pieces move on to the next step.

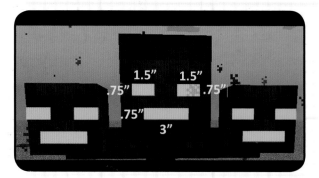

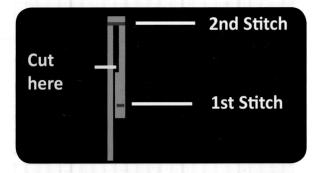

Step 5: Vicks and Biggs

In this step you are going to create the lines to help you position and attach the eyes and mouths onto each sub head.

Creating the lines

Take one of your sub head pieces and place it in front of you. The center of the crucifix is where we are going to sew the eyes and mouth. First, start by measuring up from the bottom line, on the left and right hand sides. Make a mark at 3/4" up on both sides. Draw a line across these two measurements and you will have a 3/4" gap line. Take a few push pins and push them through the line on the left, middle, and right hand sides. Once you have pushed the pins through flip the material over.

Place a ruler or another similar object behind the pins to prop them up. Pull a piece of masking tape slightly longer than the length of the face and place it flush against the three protruding pins. Slide the tape down on top of the fabric. Remove the pins and flip the material back over. Measure up from the bottom line once again and make a mark at 2 1/4" on both sides. Draw a line across both marks and push your pins through the line on the left, middle, and right sides. Flip your material back over and perk up the pins. Grab another piece of masking tape, flush

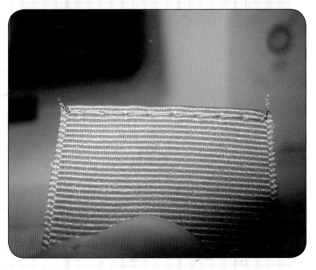

it against the pins, and slide it down on top of the fabric. Upon completion remove the pins.

Aligning the mouth

At this point you should have two rows of tape across the face area of your crucifix. Place a ruler along the bottom tape line, centering it as best as possible. Expose enough of the tape so you can put a mark on it. Now place a mouth piece on top of the ruler and split the difference on each side. As you can see in the picture, I have my ruler positioned between 15 1/16" and 19 7/16", with 10.5/16" on each side. I made both of my marks at 15 3/4" and 18 3/4", exactly 3 inches apart.

Sewing the mouth in place

Place the mouth along the top edge of the bottom tape line between both of your marks. Use a push pin, tape, or whatever method you feel comfortable with to hold the piece in place while it is being sewn. Run a stitch around the entire perimeter of the mouth piece. Once finished pull all the threads from the front of the mouth into the underside of the material. Knot and cut any excess threads.

Aligning and sewing the eyes in place

Aligning the eyes on the sub heads is a painless ordeal. Place each eye on the top edge of the upper tape line flush against the left and right sides of the head. Using a push pin or tape to hold the eyes in place, run a stitch around the entire perimeter of each eye. Once finished, pull all the threads from the front of the eye into the underside of the material. Knot and cut any excess threads.

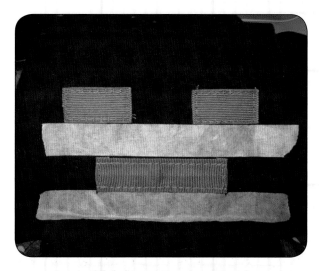

Step 6: Wedge

In this step you are going to create the lines to help you position and attach the eyes and mouth onto the main head. This step will be nearly identical to the sub heads with the only difference being the measurements.

Creating the lines

Grab your main head piece and place it in front of you. The center of the crucifix is where we are going to sew the eyes and mouth. First, start by measuring up from the bottom line, on the left and right hand sides. Make a mark at 3/4" up on both sides. Draw a line across these two measurements and you will have a 3/4" gap line. Take a few push pins and push them through the line on the left, middle, and right hand sides. Once you have pushed the pins through flip the material over.

Place a ruler or another similar object behind the pins to prop them up. Pull a piece of masking tape slightly longer than the length of the face and place it flush against the three protruding pins. Slide the tape down on top of the fabric. Remove the pins and flip the material back over. Measure up from the

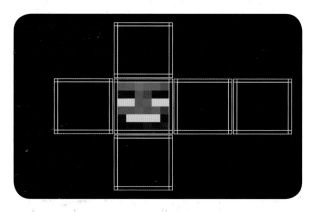

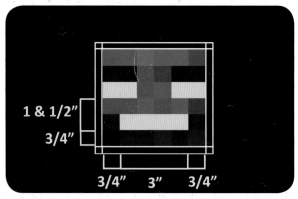

1 & 1/2"

3/4"

3/4"   3"   3/4"

bottom line once again and make a mark at 2 1/4" on both sides. Draw a line across both marks and push your pins through the line on the left, middle, and right sides. Flip your material back over and perk up the pins. Grab another piece of masking tape, flush it against the pins and slide it down on top of the fabric. Upon completion remove the pins.

Aligning the mouth

At this point you should have two rows of tape across the face area of your crucifix. Place a ruler along the bottom tape line, centering it as best as possible. Expose enough of the tape so you can put a mark on it. Now place a mouth piece on top of the ruler and split the difference on each side. As you can see in the picture I have my ruler positioned between 14 1/16" and 19 15/16" with 1 7/16" on each side. I made both of my marks at 15 1/2" and 18 1/2", exactly 3 inches apart.

Sewing the mouth in place

Place the mouth along the top edge of the bottom tape line between both of your marks. Use a push pin, tape, or whatever method you feel comfortable with to hold the piece into place while it is being sewn. Run a stitch around the entire perimeter of the mouth piece. Once finished pull all the threads from the front of the mouth into the underside of the material. Knot and cut any excess threads.

Aligning and sewing the eyes in place

Aligning the eyes on the main head is slightly different from the sub heads, but it's still a rather simple ordeal. As you have done with the bottom tape line, center your ruler on the upper line. Measuring from the fabric's outer edge, measure inward 3/4", making a mark on both the left and right sides. As you can see in the pictures I have my ruler centered between 10 1/16" and 15 15/16" with my alignment marks on 10 13/16" and 15 3/16". Flush both of the eyes to the top edge of the upper line with the outer portion of the eyes lined up against your two alignment marks. Once everything is aligned, use a push pin or tape to hold the eyes in place. Run a stitch around the entire perimeter of each eye. Then pull all the threads from the front of the eye into the underside of the material. Knot and cut any excess threads. Onward to the next step.

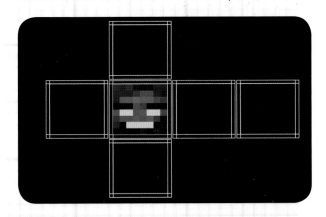

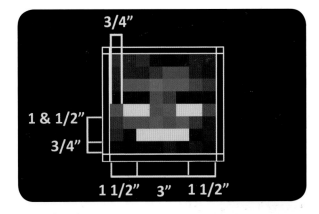

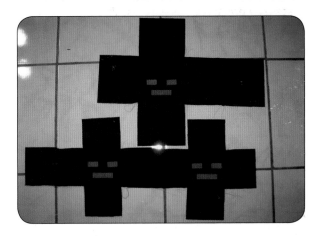

Step 7: Closing Vicks, Biggs, and Wedge

In this step you are going to completely enclose all three heads.

Sewing the head closed

Follow the colored diagram and pictures to help you close and stitch the head completely shut. Breaking down the steps, step 1 is sewing the top and bottom of the crucifix together to form a box with two open ends. Steps 2–4 are entirely closing the top of the head. Steps 5–7 is completely closing the bottom of the head.

Cutting the fill hole

After you're finished, you will cut a small hole along the bottom of the head and flip the material inside out. Liberally fill the head with FiberFill until you're satisfied with the way it feels. Don't under fill it because the FiberFill will eventually settle.

Stitching the fill hole

Looking at the detailed picture, perform a slip stitch to close the hole along the bottom of the head. When you reach the end of the hole, sew back through the material and knot the thread. Then push your needle and thread back through the piece and cut the thread. This will help hide the thread. I attached some pictures of me closing the slip stitch on a few pieces that you will have to make shortly. Insert Images

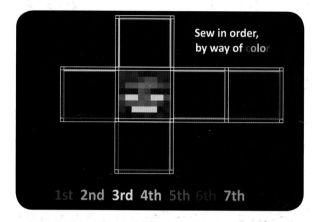

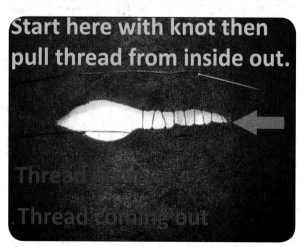

Step 8: Sewing the Torso

In this step you are going to sew the torso together and fill it with stuffing.

Sewing the torso

Gather all of your shoulder pieces and begin stitching them into place. Follow the colored diagram and pictures to help piece them all together. The arrows indicate the area where you will flip the material inside out and fill it with stuffing.

Breaking down the steps

Steps 1–5 are sewing the four torso and two end pieces together. Step 6 is folding the entire piece together to form a hollow box. Step 7 is completely shutting the end of the hollow box. Step 8 is sewing two of the three sides left open.

Sewing the torso closed

Since you have already performed the slip stitch three times already you should have no problem closing the torso. The only difference this time is that you will be folding the extra material back in on itself. Try to make it match the other three sides as best as possible. Once you are done, move on to the next step. The picture with the material folded back was pulled from a process later in the project. Your torso piece should have only one side open.

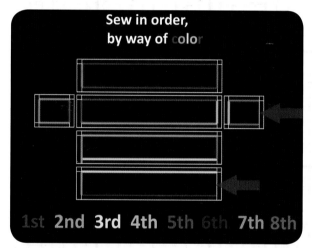

Step 9: Shouldering On

In this step you are going to create a shoulder piece for your Wither. Casual or hardcore?

Easier method

If you are going with the easier method then this process will be similar to the torso piece. Gather all of your shoulder pieces and begin stitching them into place. Follow the colored diagram and pictures to help piece them all together. The arrows indicate the area where you will flip the material inside out and fill it with stuffing.

Steps 1–5 are sewing the four shoulder and two end pieces together. Step 6 is folding the entire piece together to form a hollow box. Step 7 is completely shutting the end of the hollow box. Step 8 is sewing two of the three sides left open.

Now that your shoulder is generously filled, fold the material back in on itself and slip stitch the final remaining open end.

Harder method

Congratulations on choosing the harder method and staying truer to the actual Wither dimensions. Follow the colored diagram and look at the pictures to help you join all of the pieces together. Start with the "Sides and Bottom" diagram then move on to the "Top Section" diagram, or vice versa. Once you have both pieces you will need to join them both together.

Take a look at the colored diagram to help you see how the top and bottom sections connect to one another. You don't have to follow the colored orders precisely, however, all the areas that are colored need to be sewn. When you are done, the piece will be completely sewn shut. Cut a hole horizontally centered on top of the shoulder. Make it large enough so that you can flip the piece inside out. Fill the shoulder with FiberFill to your heart's content and then perform a slip stitch to close the seam. Move on to the next step.

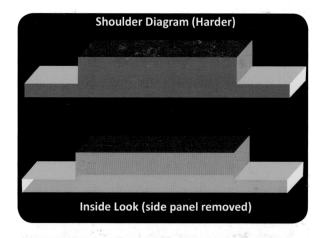

Shoulder Diagram (Harder)

Inside Look (side panel removed)

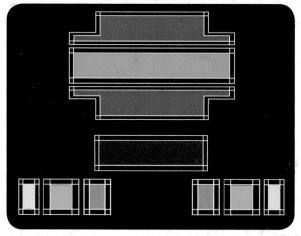

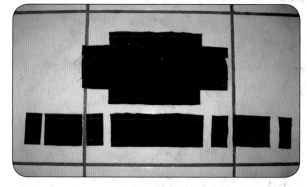

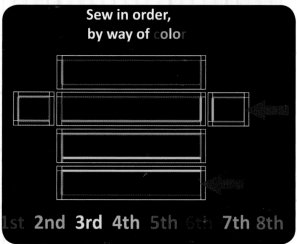

Sew in order, by way of color

1st 2nd **3rd 4th** 5th 6th **7th 8th**

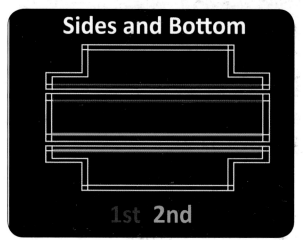

Sides and Bottom

1st **2nd**

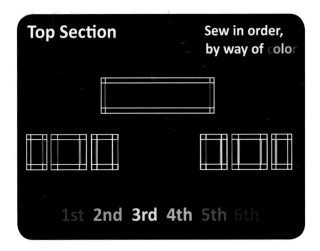

Top Section Sew in order, by way of color

1st **2nd 3rd 4th** 5th 6th

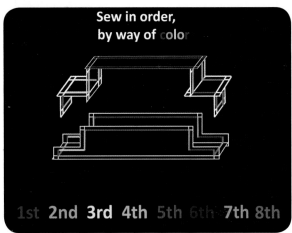

Sew in order, by way of color

1st **2nd 3rd 4th** 5th 6th **7th 8th**

Step 10: Six-Piece Riblets, Please!

In this step you're going to create the ribs for your Wither. Sewing them is exactly like the torso but on a smaller scale with more volume. Gather all of your pieces and stitch them together, leaving one end open so you can flip it inside out. I'm not sure why, but I left two seams open on the end of each rib. Honestly, I should have only left one. This would have helped cut down on the hand sewing. Just as you have done with the torso, fill each rib with an adequate amount of fill and close the end with a slip stitch.

Step 11: Sewing It All Together

You've reached "The End" but there's no Dragon Egg, only more work! The first picture depicts all of the areas that are going to be sewn in this entire step.
Attaching the sub heads

Look at the pictures to get a good idea of how far the sub head will hang off the back of the shoulder. The actual dimensions are 1/2 of a block, which would equate to 3/8" in 75 percent dimensions. I personally didn't measure it out, but for the sake of the Instructable it must be mentioned. Now place a sub head on one side of the shoulder. On the top corner edge of the

rear shoulder, thread and tie a knot. Sew a slip stitch between the seam and the head, working your way towards the middle. If you chose the harder method, it helps to leave a decent amount of slack in the stitch before tightening it up. This will help you get your needle in the tight space between the head and inner shoulder. Once you reach the corner, knot the thread, push the needle back through the piece, and cut off the excess.

Next, flip the shoulder piece around and run a slip stitch along the front side. After you're done with that, stitch the inner portion of the head onto the shoulder. Great job, now you get to sew on the other sub head.
Attaching the main head

Before you sew on the main head I would recommend that you find the center point of the bottom front and rear portions of the head as well as the center point of the shoulder. This will help ensure a perfect alignment of the head. You may use a Sharpie to make a small mark or you can use a push pin to mark the center. Align the main head between the two sub heads and sew it along the bottom front and rear portions of the head.
Attaching the ribs to the torso

The ribs lie 1 1/2 blocks down from the top of the torso. In 75 percent terms, that means it's 1.125" from the top, or 1 1/8". Measure down from the top of the torso and make a mark. Now, take one of the ribs and thread a needle through the top corner edge of an end piece. Tie a knot then align it with the mark on the torso, centering it on the side in which it sits. Slip stitch around the entire rib, mating it to the torso. There is one block of space between each rib, or 3/4" in 75 percent terms. You may measure the distance between each one or just use the all-mighty "eye ball-it" method. Once you sew on the first rib you may find it difficult to sew the next one below it. To alleviate this quagmire, leave the slip stitch loose until you're about halfway around. This will help give you plenty of room to maneuver your hand between the two ribs.
Attaching the torso to the shoulder

You are but one last stitch from completing the Wither. Center the completed torso with the shoulder. Feel free to measure each piece and find the center for a perfect alignment. Slip stitch around the entire perimeter of the top portion of the torso, mating it to the shoulder.

Mission accomplished! You've done it! Now run around the house with it like you're attacking livestock. PEWWW, PEWWW, PEWWWWWWWWW . . . BOOOOOOSHHHHHHH!!!!! Your (wife/husband/kids/parents/grandparents/friends/mail delivery guy/creepy neighbor looking through the window) totally saw you doing that!

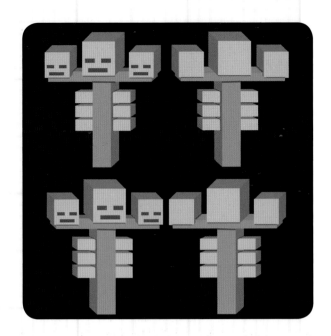

Stuffed Creeper Doll

Dylan Buchanan

(http://www.instructables.com/id/Minecraft-Stuffed-Creeper-Doll/)

Need a project for when you're away from your crafting table (computer desk)? Bring a bit of the Minecraft world into real life with a cuddly little creeper pal!

The creeper's blocky geometric shape makes this a great beginner project for people unfamiliar with sewing. Also it's your best shot at giving a creeper a hug without it costing you the north wall of your house.

Step 1: That's a Very Nice EVERYTHING You Have There...

- Ruler
- Erasable marker—you can find one made especially for fabric at any craft store
- Fabric shears – a.k.a. a big ol' pair of scissors
- Sewing needle
- Pins
    Materials:
- Green fabric (fleece is good) – About half a yard should do; go to the fabric store if you don't feel like punching sheep and cooking cacti
- Matching spool of thread
- FiberFill/Stuffing
- Either black embroidery thread or black fabric scraps

Step 2: Anatomy of a Creeper

Thankfully, Minecraft's pixelated graphics and geometric shapes make the creeper one of the easiest patterns you will find. For my pattern I translated every two pixels into one inch.

Head: 4" x 4" x 4"
Body: 2" x 4" x 6"

Legs: 2" x 2" x 3"—make four of these

Map out the panels for each side of these boxes on your fabric. Be sure to keep about a half inch allowance around the edges of each outline. Keep in mind that you do not need to cut out the top side of the body because it is closed off by the creeper's head.

When you cut the pieces out do not cut along the lines you drew. Instead, cut about a half-inch to a quarter-inch outside the line.

The pieces should be easy to recognize, but if you think you will have trouble mixing them up I suggest labeling each part or cutting out only the pieces of the section you are working on.

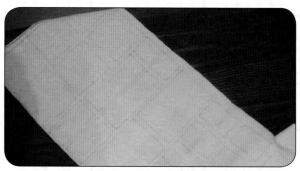

Step 3: Pinning

Each body part is essentially a box consisting of six pieces: the top, bottom, and four sides, except for the body which has no top.

First, line up the sides of two pieces of a body part and pin them together where they will be attached. Be sure to pin them together with the lines you drew facing out.

Step 4: Stitching

Thread your needle.

For those of you unfamiliar with sewing, you do this by feeding the thread through the eye of the needle. After cutting off a length of thread, tie the two ends together with a large knot. This is done essentially by tying several knots in one spot.

To start stitching, push the needle through the two pieces of fabric at the corner you drew on. Make sure the needle comes out at the same corner on the other side. From that side, push the needle back through the fabric a little bit down the line. Again, make sure it comes out the other side on the line. Continue like this down the line, removing the pins as you go. This is a basic running stitch.

Make sure to double back on the first stitch of any new piece of thread to keep it anchored securely.

When you reach the end of your seam, double back once to create a loop. Feed the needle and thread through the loop and pull it tight to anchor. For added security, do this twice before cutting off the excess thread.

Step 5: Form the Legs

Use the running stitch to sew together the four sides of the leg. When you have those together, pin the top panel in place and start stitching around the top until it's secured to all four sides.

Flip it over and pin down the last remaining piece. This time only stitch around three sides, leaving the last seam open.

Step 6: Om Nom Nom

By now you should have all but one seam done on the leg. Turn it inside out through the open side.

Take a handful of FiberFill and stuff the leg part until it's nice and plush. Pay attention to stuffing the corners so they puff out into the desired blocky shape.

Fold in the edges of the open seam.

Step 7: The Slip Stitch

With the leg stuffed it is time to close up the last remaining seam. For this you will use a slip stitch, which is invisible from the outside.

Start your thread from the inside of the fold of one side. Go across to the other side and prick the needle in and back out again, catching a little fabric along the edge of the fold. Go back across and do the same on the other edge, lining up where the needle goes in with where it came out on the last fold.

Continue down to the end and tie off the thread.

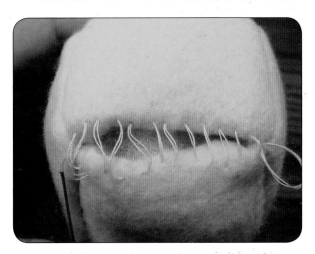

Step 8: The Face

The head is assembled the same way as the legs.

For my creeper I decided to embroider on the face. This part could be difficult for beginners, who might prefer just to stitch on some black patches in the shape of the eyes and mouth. A third, even simpler option would be to use fabric glue, which you could probably purchase wherever you found your fabric.

Patching the face

I'm afraid I don't have pictures but hopefully this will explain it.

Start by drawing out the outline of the face on the black fabric (it could be difficult to see on black; be sure you will be able to spot your line while you work). Cut around the shapes of the eyes and mouth, leaving about a half-inch to a quarter-inch space between the cut edge and the line you drew. Fold in the edges along the lines. If your marker will clean off easily or is camouflaged by the black fabric, fold with the lines on the outside. If the lines will show, fold with them inside.

With the edges folded in, this is what the patch will look like on the front of the head.

Arrange the patches on the face of your head cube and pin them down. Be sure to pin the folds in place while you are pinning the whole patch to the head. Now you should easily be able to perform a slip stitch between the folded edges (along the line if you can see it) and the green fabric directly below it. When you are done there should be no loose fabric edges sticking out and hopefully no visible stitching.

Embroidering the face

If you are feeling adventurous enough, get yourself some embroidery thread and a needle.

Start by mapping out the face on one side of the cube.

Embroidery works best when the fabric is stretched out as you work on it. Had I thought ahead I probably would have added the face before I even cut out the pieces. What I wound up doing instead was rigging up a cardboard frame to hold the face taut from the inside.

To ready your needle, cut a length of embroidery thread. It usually comes as six or so threads bunched together. Separate one or two of these threads and use them to thread your needle. An embroidery needle is a special needle with a larger eye to accommodate the extra thread.

Starting from the inside of the head, feed the needle out at the top of the eye and back in at the bottom, trailing the thread down the outside. Poke the needle back out along the line right next to where the thread goes in at the bottom of the eye, sticking it back in at the top, next to where the thread comes out. Repeat, working your way down the eye until the eye is properly filled in. Tie off the thread on the inside of the head. Make sure not to pull the thread too tight or your face will wind up scrunched up.

Do the same to fill in the other eye and mouth. This will take some patience and a steady hand.

When the head is ready, stuff it with FiberFill and close it up as you did with the legs.

Step 9: Stuffing the Body

The body stitches together the same as the legs and head except it only has five sides. Instead of having a top panel it will be stitched directly to the head to close it off.

Draw a 2" x 4" outline at the center of the bottom of the head. Use this box as the top panel of the body. Using the slip stitch, sew three sides of the body to the head along the line, leaving the back open.

Stuff the body with FiberFill through the opening and stitch it closed.

Step 10: Assemble the Parts on Your Crafting Table

The legs are attached to the body simply with a slip stitch at the edges of the legs and body. When they are tightly secured your creeper is ready for cuddlin'.

Step 11: SSSSSSsssssssssss...

Now run like hell.

Pig USB Holder

sylrig
(http://www.instructables.com/id/Fill-a-Minecraft-Pig-with-Minecraft/)

Fill a Minecraft pig with Minecraft—or anything else you want to put onto a flash drive. The drive hides in leg of this paper-and-Styrofoam Minecraft pig.

Step 1: Tools and Materials

- Cardstock to print the papercraft pig onto
- Scissors
- Paper adhesive (we used both a glue stick and a hot glue gun)
- Solid Styrofoam packing (not peanuts)
- Serrated blade for cutting the Styrofoam
- A sharp point, such as a nail or a toothpick
- Pencil
- An Xacto knife or other sharp blade
- A tiny flash drive

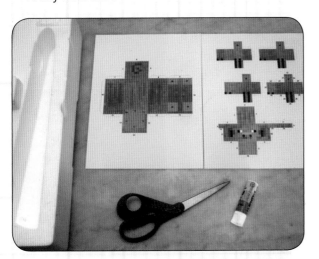

Step 2: Cut the Pig and Styrofoam

Cut out the pattern, being sure to keep the tabs. Crease all sides and tabs.

Use the pattern to measure and cut blocks of Styrofoam, which will be glued inside the cardstock. The sawing motion of the serrated blade makes it easier to get a relatively straight cut.

Step 3: Glue Cardstock around the Styrofoam

With the Styrofoam cut to size, glue the creased cardstock pieces around it.

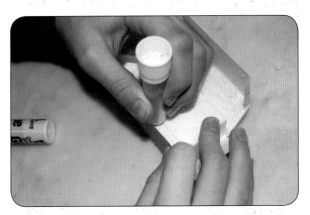

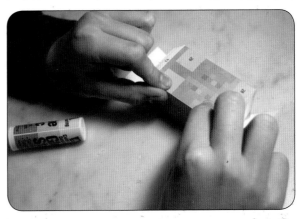

Step 4: The Head

The head is slightly irregular. It's easiest to make a cube first, then notch out the part that will not be covered by cardstock.

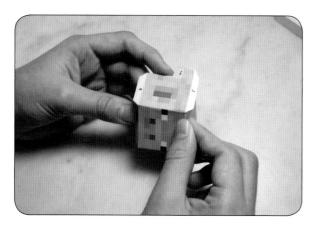

Step 6: Fitting the Pig Together

Using the end of the flash drive, trace and cut a slot in the body with the Xacto. The leg should now fit snugly into the body.

Attach the other legs and head using the hot glue gun.

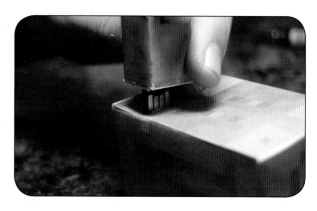

Step 5: Fitting the Flash Drive

With a nail or other sharp implement, hollow out one of the legs in the shape of the flash drive. Trace a slot for the drive on the back side of the cardstock and cut it out carefully with your Xacto blade.

After fitting the drive snugly into the Styrofoam, glue the leg around the foam as usual, being careful to fit around the drive.

Step 7: Use Your Pig

Remember to load the drive with your Minecraft game or whatever else you want to keep on it. It will stay hidden within your pig.

Minecraft Fashion/Wearables

Fingerless Gloves

Creeper Hat

Mooshroom Hat

Enderman Hat

Creeper Costume

Steve Costume

Fingerless Gloves

Holly Beth Mann

(http://www.instructables.com/id/Minecraft-Creeper-Fingerless-Gloves-Pattern/)

Minecraft is so popular now so I made my son some fingerless gloves with the Minecraft Creeper on them! They are very easy to make and do not take long at all.

Step 1: Materials Needed

- Polar fleece or other fleece-like material for the glove. If you use some type of fleece, it's simple because you don't need to sew the edges under as they don't unravel. (I didn't have black fleece material so I used a soft black material and had to sew edges under)
- Scissors or rotary cutter
- Sewing machine or needle and thread
- Printer—you'll need to print out the pattern pieces (you can download the PDF pattern on instructabes.)

Step 2: Instructions

Print out the pattern pieces. The pattern included here is what I would call a size small. It fits my son, who is almost 8 years old, comfortably, and it also fits me. If you want to be sure about the sizing, the small measures approximately 7 1/2 inches around the palm of the hand underneath the fingers (the part of the fingerless glove where the top connects with the thumb area—measuring all the way around and back to that point). If you would like to increase the size to a medium, you can print out the pattern and add 1/2 an inch on both sides, and add an inch to make it a large. It may take some practice to get your right size, but if you plan on making more gloves it is nice to have some that fit well.

Cutting the fabric.

Be sure to lay out the fabric so that the direction of the stretch is horizontal to your project so it allows for some stretching and room for your hands. You can fold your fabric and lay out your pattern piece, pin it, then cut it out and repeat. For the Minecraft creeper piece, you should cut out the piece from green felt. I had to take the actual paper pattern piece for the creeper and use some small scissors to cut the square face pieces out. The material for my gloves were black, so I needed to cut out those pieces from the green felt so the black material would show through.

Preparing the cut fabric.

If your fabric has a dull side, make sure that is on the outside now—so after you sew it, turn it right-side out—the non-dull side will be showing on your finished product.

Sewing on the creeper.

I recommend that you lay the creeper onto the fabric and try to figure out where you want it to be sewn on exactly (see my pictures for a reference). Then pin it onto the black material. You may need to trim a little on the side. I recommend that you either sew it on by hand or use a zigzag stitch of some sort on your sewing machine to carefully sew it on. It's not the easiest thing to do, but it also doesn't need to be perfect. The only time I had any issues was when going around edges or corners with the zigzag stitches, but if you take your time there, it'll turn out really nice. Once that is done, you can sew the seams together to finish up the glove.

Sewing the seams.

I recommend a 1/4" seam allowance on all sides except for the thumb seam. Gradually decrease the seam size once you near the thumb area to a 1/8" seam allowance. Be careful to reinforce the stitches by going back and forth or going over the entire seam twice. It is up to you. No need to sew the top or bottom of the gloves—the fleece will not fray.

Shortening the thumb.

Everyone's hands are different. If the thumb slot is too long, use your scissors (carefully) or rotary cutter to slice a piece off to shorten it. Be sure to go over your stitches again.

Finishing touches.

You can trim the excess seam or leave it as is. If you trim it, use a rotary cutter to be safe and do not cut too close to your seam. If you don't do that, it is fine too—just be sure to cut little half triangles out of the seam bottoms so your seam does not poke out.

Turn the gloves right-side out and you are done!

Creeper Hat

Lydia Sedy

(http://www.instructables.com/id/Minecraft-Creeper-Hat/)

Show your Minecraft pride and make a Creeper hat! This hat is easy, fun, and will definitely get you into your creative mode.

Step 1: Materials

- At least 1/3 yard of green fleece
- Some black fleece (about 5" x 5")
- The pattern below. It's fairly easy enough to make your own if needed
- A kitty companion

Step 2: Cutting Everything Out

You can download the pattern on Instructables or freehand draw your own. The most important things are making sure it's wide enough on the bottom edge (mine is 11 1/2") and that it's symmetrical.

For the face, it's important to make sure your lines are straight and you have right angles. Using graph paper as a pattern will make this so much easier! You can use the pattern in the fourth picture or make your own.

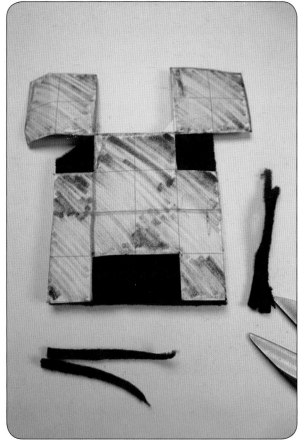

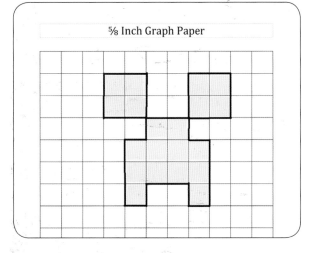

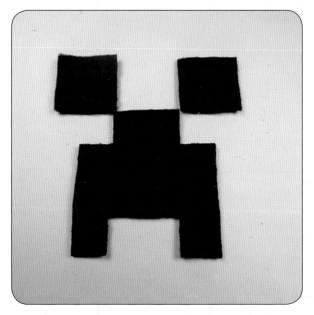

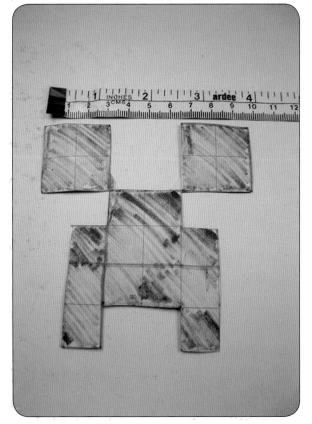

⅝ Inch Graph Paper

Step 3: Putting Darts in the Top of the Hat

Take each part of the green pieces and fold them in half, hot dog style, with the right sides in. At the very top, measure two inches down and mark with a pin. About 1/2" over from the fold on the top, draw a diagonal line with a piece of chalk down to the pin you marked (first picture). Sew along this line to make a dart, decreasing the size of the top (pictures 3 and 4).

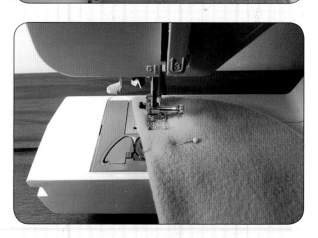

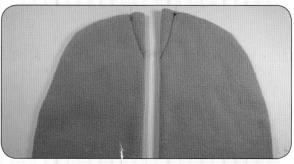

Step 4: Sewing the Hat Together

Take both sides and match the darts at the top, pinning with the right sides in. Match the sides all around and pin as well. Sew along the entire edge. If you want a nicer look on the inside, you can finish the edge with an over-stitch.

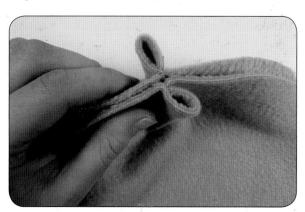

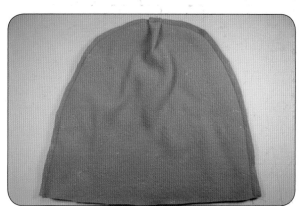

Step 5: Sew Up the Brim

Keep the hat inside out and try it on. Fold the excess fabric up to your desired length. Using a mirror, pin the brim so you can keep the placement. Be careful not to poke yourself!

Once you have the hat off, measure where you pinned and make sure it's the same all the way around the hat, pinning as you go. Sew all the way around.

Turn it right side out and you have finished the basic hat!

Step 6: Sew on the Face

Place the mouth on the front of the hat and pin in place. Sew all the way around, picking up the foot to turn at the corners. Do the same with the eyes. Be sure to clip away any extra threads and uneven edges. You have finished your hat!

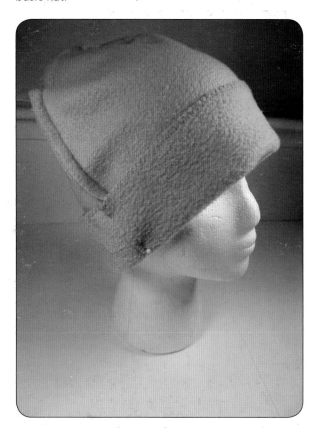

Mooshroom Hat

Teisha J. Rowland

(http://www.instructables.com/id/The-Mooshroom-Hat/)

For everybody who's ever wanted to wear a Minecraft Mooshroom on their head (or knows somebody who'd love a Mooshroom hat as a gift), this Instructables project is for you! (And really, who wouldn't want to wear a giant, red, fungus-ridden cow on their head?) It's a definite attention-getter at any convention. I was inspired to do this because I made a light-up Christmas tree hat that was really popular, and I figured that if people liked wearing a lit-up tree on their head, then they wouldn't mind wearing a cow there either. And, it's probably obvious that I really enjoy Minecraft—I also made a Minecraft-themed candle-powered paper carousel.

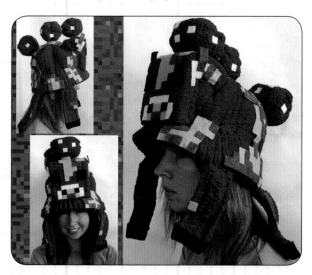

Step 1: Materials You'll Need

- Martha Stewart Crafts Knit & Weave Loom Kit. I used this specific loom/knitting kit because I won it in a contest, but you could probably use a different kit and adjust it to work (or, if you're experienced at knitting, you could probably knit all of this without a kit). See the details in the steps for what loom pieces are needed.
- Red yarn, super bulky (size 6). I used Bernat Blanket Soft & Cozy yarn (Cranberry 10705) because it was the closest in color that I could find at my local yarn shop. Any super bulky, mooshroom-colored yarn should work. The ball was 234m, and I ended up needing a tiny bit from a second ball, but if you made the hat shorter you probably wouldn't need a second ball.
- Scissors
- Piece of cardboard, at least 20 cm by 12 cm

- Tape
- Utility knife
- Printer and paper
- Glue for fabric and felt. I used Elmer's Craft Bond Tacky Glue and it worked really well.
- Felt in the following colors: black, white, pink, light gray, dark gray. Get one sheet of the black, white, and pink, and two sheets of light gray and dark gray each.
- Sewing pins and paperclips. This is for holding pieces in place before gluing them.
- For gluing: heavy books (e.g., textbooks), paperback novels, binder clips, and sheets of paper (to protect the books from the glue).
- Ruler
- Polyester FiberFill
- Cardboard toilet paper tube or paper towel tube
- Somebody to laugh at you when you wear the hat!

Step 2: Knitting the Hat Base

Assembling the loom

Connect the loom pieces to form a long oval using four of the 12-hole, straight pieces and two of the 28-hole, semi-circular pieces. Insert a green peg into a hole (marking the start of the round) and then put a pink peg into every other hole going around the loom. See the pictures for details. (The booklet that came with the kit said this arrangement should make a hat with a circumference of 46 cm, which can stretch to fit a range of sizes, but mine was a bit larger. If you want it on the smaller size, you could try a smaller loom arrangement.)

Casting on

Make a slipknot and put it on the green peg. Then do an "e-wrap" around the pink peg to the left of the green peg (going clockwise around the loom). The e-wrap technique looks like a lower case "e" as it goes around the pegs. Specifically, you'll want to move the yarn inside of the loom, then go clockwise completely around the pink peg, and end up with the yarn back inside of the loom. Keep doing this for each peg, going clockwise around the loom (until you get back to the beginning, at the green peg). See the pictures for details. Be sure not to wrap the yarn too tight or it'll be hard to knit with later! For tips on knitting on a loom, check out this Loom Knitting: Getting Started on the Round Loom PDF. Go around the loom using the e-wrap two more times, so each peg should have three wraps of yarn around it. (You should end back up at the green peg.)

Tip: If you're new to using a knitting loom, you may want to practice a few rounds of e-stitches to make sure you're happy with how tight/loose your stitches are.

Knitting stitches

I used the one-over-two stitch technique because I liked the appearance it gave for this hat. Once you

137

have three loops of yarn on each peg, do the one-over-two stitch by hooking the knitting tool (with the metal hook) under the bottom loop of yarn on the green peg, and then carefully lift it over the peg. The green peg should now have two loops of yarn. See the pictures for details. Continue to do this to each peg, going clockwise around the loom. You should end up with two loops on each peg (stop at the green peg). Your first round has now been knitted!

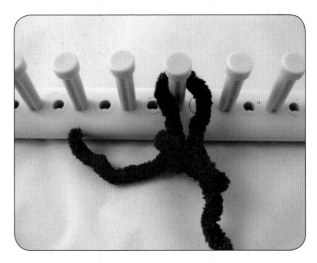

Now do the e-stitch for one complete round on the loom, going clockwise around it. Each peg should now have three loops of yarn on it again. Repeat this one-over-two stitch until you have completed 50 rounds. If you want a shorter hat than what's pictured, you could stop before 50 rounds.

Binding off

Knit off a round of stitches so that you're left with only one loop of yarn on each peg. Cut the yarn so that the loom is left with a length that's almost twice the circumference of the loom itself. Then take the knitting needle and thread this yarn tail into it. Starting at the green peg, put the needle through the yarn on the peg and pull the yarn through. Continue moving the needle through the yarn on each peg, going clockwise around the loom. Stop when you get back to the green peg.

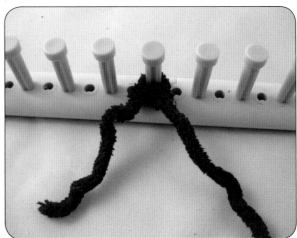

Use the knitting tool to remove the last loop of yarn from each peg, lifting the yarn over the peg as you did before. Gently pull on the tail of yarn to close the end of the hat. Then flip the hat inside-out, so the knitted "rows" are on the inside (and the flatter side is on the outside).

Finishing touches

To adjust the hat length and give the hat a cute brim, you can fold the last few inches up and over the bottom of the hat—see the pictures. Take a new piece of yarn that's a little longer than the circumference of the hat and use it to attach the folded-over edge in place (sewing together what was the end of the hat with the main part of the hat). You can also use this yarn to adjust the circumference of the hat so that it fits you well. To do this, collect the ends of the yarn on one side of the hat (this will be its back), try the hat on, and pull the yarn until the hat feels snug. Then you can tie the yarn together to keep the circumference consistent. See the pictures for details.

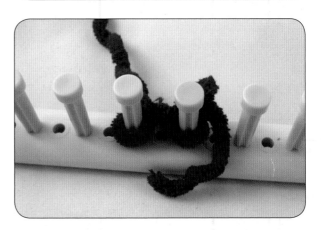

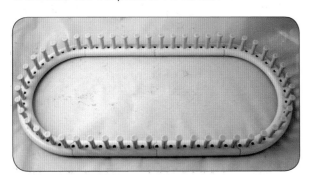

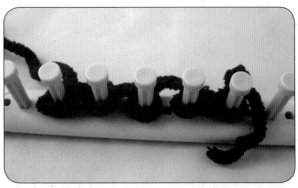

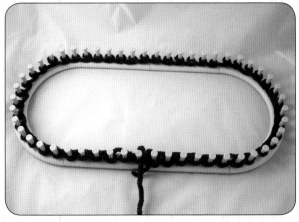

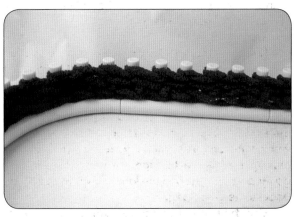

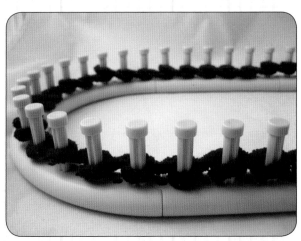

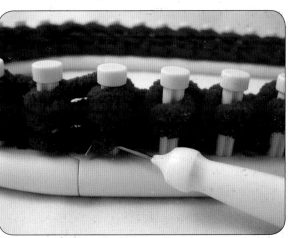

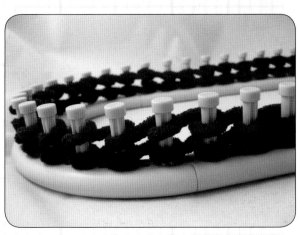

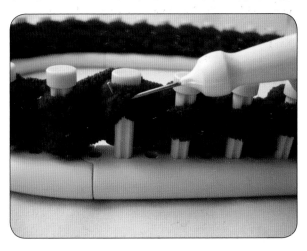

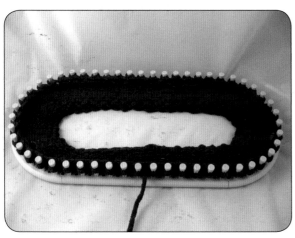 

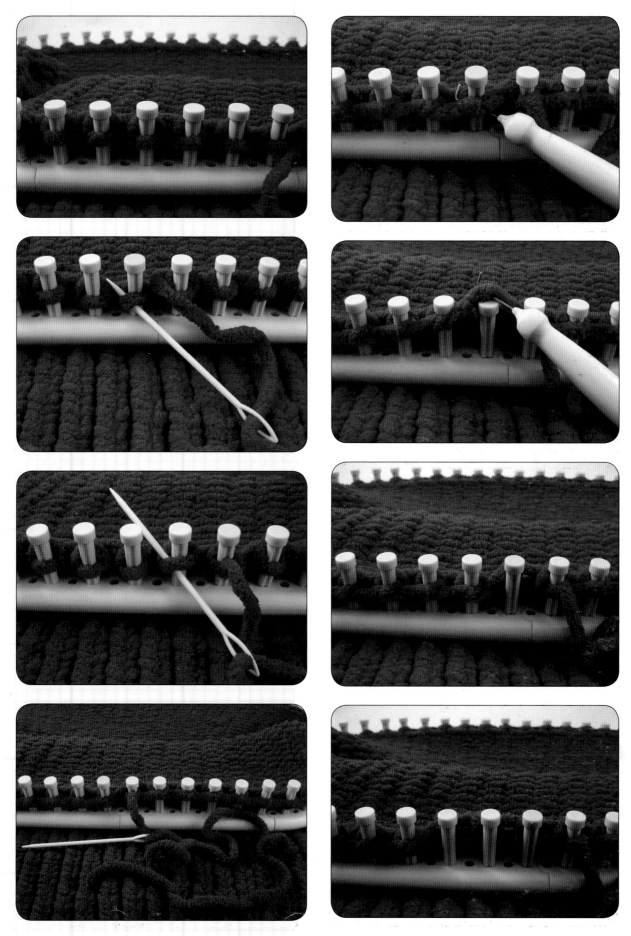

the tail is, put the needle through the yarn on the peg and pull the yarn through. Continue moving the needle through the yarn on each peg. Stop when you get back to the end of the row. Use the knitting tool to remove the last loop of yarn from each peg, lifting the yarn over the peg as you did before.

Making the other legs

Repeat this step three more times to knit a total of four legs.

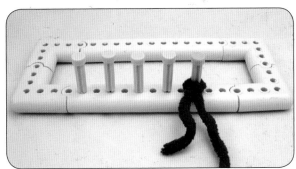

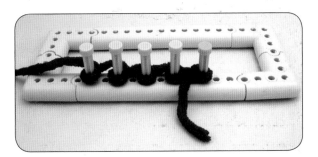

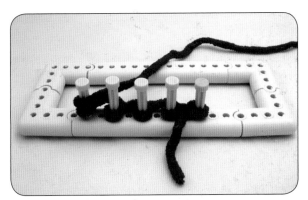

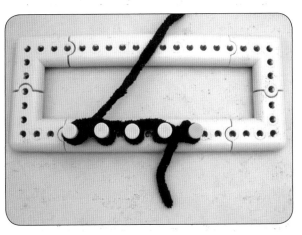

Step 3: Knitting the Legs

Assembling the loom

Connect the loom pieces to form a rectangle using two 12-hole, straight pieces and four 6-hole, corner pieces. (The rectangle shape is just to give the loom more structure—you'll only be using part of one side of it.) Insert a green peg into a hole (marking the start of the round) and then put four pink pegs into every other hole on the left of the green peg (making five pegs in the loom in total). See the pictures for details.

Casting on

Make a slipknot and put it on the green peg. Then do an e-wrap (as described in Step 2) around each pink peg, moving to the left on the loom. When you get to the last pink peg, do a second e-wrap loop around it, ending up with your yarn back inside of the loom. Then move the yarn clockwise around the peg to the right, and continue doing this (moving right across the loom) until you reach the green peg. The two loops on each peg should be right on top of each other. See the pictures for details (as this can be confusing!). Then do an e-wrap around each peg again, ending up on the far left pink peg with three loops of yarn on each peg.

Knitting stitches

Use the one-over-two stitch technique (as described in Step 2) to knit 30 rounds on the loom. Each "round" will be when you end up on the right-most or left-most peg, since you're not knitting in a circle (or you can think of a "round" as being when you have used the knitting tool to lift a loop of yarn over each peg on the row).

Binding off

Knit off a round of stitches so that you're left with only one loop of yarn on each peg. Cut the yarn so that the loom is left with a length that's the length of the loom itself. Then take the knitting needle and thread this yarn tail into it. Starting at the end where

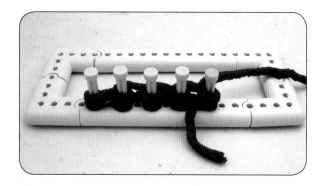

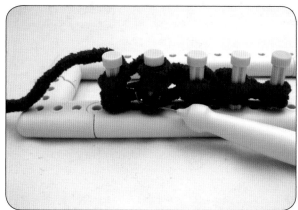

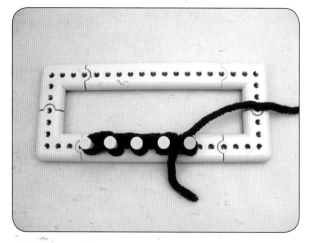

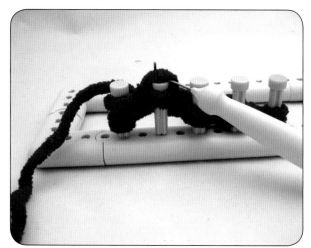

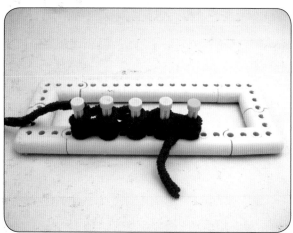

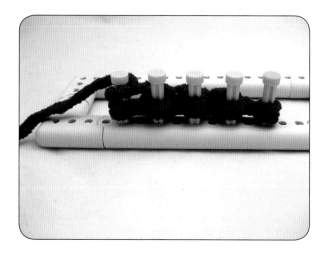

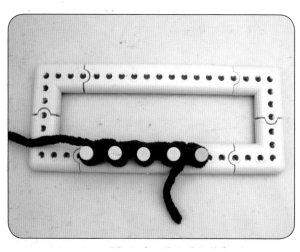

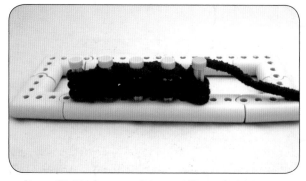

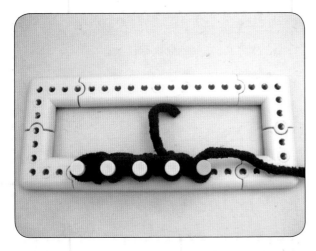

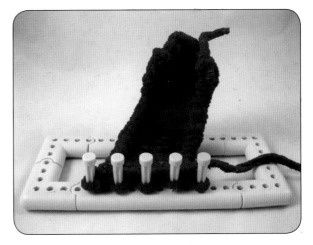

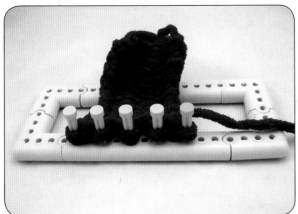

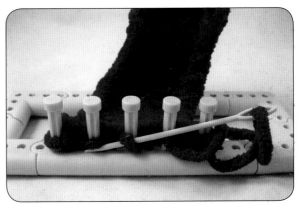

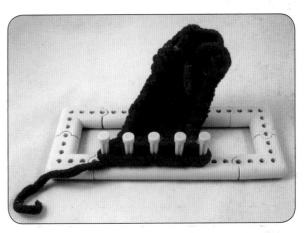

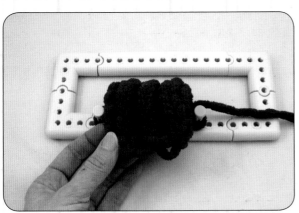

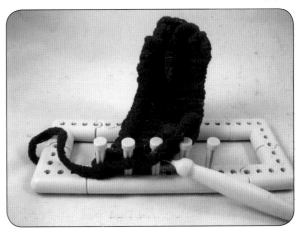

Step 4: Knitting the Head

Assembling the loom

Connect the loom pieces to form a long rectangle using two 36-hole, straight pieces and four 6-hole, corner pieces. (The rectangle shape is just to give the loom more structure—you'll only be using part of one side of it.) Insert a green peg into a hole (marking the start of the round) and then put 13 pink pegs into every other hole on the left of the green peg (making 14 pegs in the loom in total). See the pictures for details.

Casting on

Do this as you did in Step 3. You should end up with three loops of yarn on each peg.

Knitting stitches

Use the one-over-two stitch technique (as described in Step 2) to knit 38 rounds on the loom. Each "round" will be when you end up on the right-most or left-most peg, since you're not knitting in a circle (or you can think of a "round" as being when you have used the knitting tool to lift a loop of yarn over each peg on the row).

Binding off

Knit off a round of stitches so that you're left with only one loop of yarn on each peg. Cut the yarn so that the loom is left with a length that's the length of the loom itself. Then take the knitting needle and thread this yarn tail into it. Starting at the end where the tail is, put the needle through the yarn on the peg and pull the yarn through. Continue moving the needle through the yarn on each peg. Stop when you get back to the end of the row. Use the knitting tool to remove the last loop of yarn from each peg, lifting the yarn over the peg as you did before.

Attaching the face to cardboard

You should end up with a knitted square that's about 20 cm in width. This will be attached to a piece of cardboard that will make a firm head. Cut a piece of cardboard that is 20 cm by 11.5 cm. On the cardboard, make a straight line that is 11.5 cm from one of the short ends (and make the line parallel to that end). Use a utility knife to carefully cut through one layer of the cardboard, leaving the other layer intact. Bend the cut cardboard pieces back so that they form a 90° angle. Then use a few pieces of tape to hold the cardboard in place at 90°. See the pictures for details. Use scissors (or a utility knife) to make small holes around the edge of the cardboard; see the pictures for details. Center the knitted face on the cardboard, with an end of the face reaching each short end of the cardboard, and a little bit of face going past the long sides of the cardboard. Then take a long piece of yarn and sew the face onto the cardboard using the yarn, going into the holes in the cardboard and through the knitted face. Sew all around the edge of the cardboard.

Step 5: Cutting Out and Gluing the Squares Together

Now you'll get to cut out and glue together the squares that go on the mooshroom—these are the gray patches on its body, as well as its facial features, hooves, horns, ears, udder, and the spots on the mushrooms on its back. (Each square is like a pixel.) Based on the size of head I wanted to make, I ended up making each square be about 1.55 cm by 1.55 cm. I then stared at far too many pictures of mooshrooms to figure out the exact shape (combination of squares) and colors of each non-red spot on their bodies. (Technically there are three shades of gray on their bodies, but I simplified this to two. You're welcome to add more if you want.)

Cutting out the squares

Print out the PDFs in this step. (Only the single-page PDFs—the multi-page PDF comes later.) This includes five, single-paged PDFs with shapes that are labeled A to O (first PDF), P to W (second PDF), X to Y (third PDF), Z to AF (fourth PDF), and AG to AJ (fifth PDF). Each picture should be printed out on a standard-sized sheet of paper. Carefully cut out each labeled piece (e.g., A, B, C). Then temporarily attach the paper to the same-colored felt using sewing pins or something similar (see the pictures). (The possible colors are black, white, light gray, dark gray, and pink.) Carefully cut the fabric out around the paper pieces. You will need to cut out multiple copies of some pieces. These will have a number next to them, for example: (x15). This would mean you'd need to cut 15 copies of this piece out of felt. After cutting out each felt piece, I recommend leaving the paper template stacked on top of it so you can easily remember which lettered piece it is later.

Gluing the squares together

Once you've cut all the felt pieces out, arrange them together to make the correct patches (and other features) that go on the mooshroom. To do this, refer to the five-page PDF (which should be labeled mushroom_squares_layout.pdf). This PDF shows how to arrange each felt piece on/near the other felt pieces. For example, on the first page you can see that piece F goes on top of piece E (and how they fit together), while the A pieces (the eyes) do not go on top of any other pieces. For more complicated pieces, I recommend using sewing pins to hold the pieces in place as you arrange them. Once you're happy with the arrangement of a piece, glue the individual pieces down using the tacky glue. I put a generous amount of glue on the back of each piece because I was paranoid it wouldn't hold well, but it did! Apply pressure to hold the pieces together as they glue—specifically, for larger pieces I'd recommend leaving some large, flat, heavy books on the pieces for 30-plus minutes to make sure they're securely attached.

Tip: If any visible glue residue is left, you can get rid of it by gently dabbing with a damp rag (but be sure not to get it too wet since water dissolves the glue).

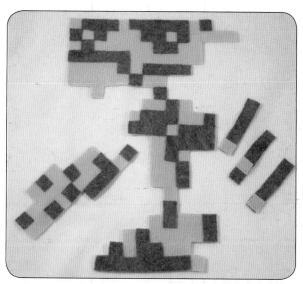

Step 6: Gluing the Squares to the Head

Arranging the pieces

Arrange the pieces on the cow's face based on the five-page PDF in Step 5. (You can also look at the pictures of the face in this step.) Pull back the parts of the knitted face that are hanging past the edges of the cardboard to create the left and right sides of the face—ears, horns, and other side-face features will go here. Pulling these sides back will turn the front into a square-shaped face. The shorter part of the head (with the smaller cardboard segment) will become the top of the head (which pieces E and F will fold back onto). See the pictures here for details.

Gluing the pieces

When you're happy with your arrangement, glue the pieces onto the head/face, one side at a time. When gluing the felt pieces onto the knitted parts, I think it's best to apply a lot of pressure for at least 30 minutes. To do this, I squeezed some novels onto the head piece between the side pieces of tape. I stacked several novels and then a textbook onto the head pieces while felt pieces were being glued to it.

Step 7: Gluing the Squares to the Hat Base

Arranging the pieces

Arrange the pieces on the cow's body based on the five-page PDF in Step 5 and based on images of mooshrooms. The reality is that the hat is not the same size/shape as a mooshroom, so you'll have to be creative while still trying to keep it similar to the real thing. I think it's best to figure out where/how you want to place the head, and then go from there. Note that the pieces around the head (L, P, and Y) may have parts of them covered by the head; this is completely fine to do. You can also look at the images in this step to see how I arranged the pieces. Here are some good mooshroom images I found that may

be helpful for placing the pieces: mooshrooms from the front, their right side, and posterior; mooshroom from the front and its right side; mooshroom from the front and its left side. I highly recommend using sewing pins (or something similar) to keep the pieces in place on the hat base as you arrange them.

Gluing the pieces

Again, as with the head, I recommend applying a lot of pressure for at least 30 minutes when gluing the felt pieces onto the knitted parts. Also, only do one side/piece at a time. To do this I basically flattened out one part of the hat at a time as I glued the pieces on. I flattened it in a sandwich of sheets of paper and then textbooks (the paper was to protect the textbooks from the glue).

Tip: To glue the back pieces on the mooshroom, I squeezed paperback novels in there to make a flat gluing surface out of its back.

Step 8: Gluing the Squares to the Legs
Gluing the pieces
The J/O pieces should go on the right legs while the J/K pieces should go on the left legs. The J/O pieces should go about halfway up the legs, along the front edge. The J/K pieces should go near the top of the legs, along the front edge. See the pictures (and mooshroom linked images in Step 7) for details. Glue the pieces as described in Step 7. The AJ pieces (large, black rectangles) are the hooves. Fold the hooves over the bottom of each leg, as shown in the pictures here. There should be a little extra felt on the left and right sides of each hoof. Glue the hooves on like this. Once they have dried, take the extra felt edges, pin them together (if necessary), and fold them backwards. Glue them backwards like this (so the extra felt is on the back sides of the legs), using a binder clip to hold them while they glue.

Arranging the legs on the body
Figure out where the legs should go—again you can use mooshroom images (linked in Step 7) or the pictures here to see where the legs go relative to the head, specific patches, and other features. I recommend basically placing them symmetrically (on the left and right sides of the body, back from the head) and not too far forward that they get in the way of peripheral vision.

Attaching the legs
Use the yarn tail of the legs (if available) to sew them onto the edge of the hat. (If there isn't a tail available, just use a new piece of yarn.)

Step 9: Knitting the Mushrooms
Assembling the loom
Connect the loom pieces to form a small rectangle using two 6-hole, straight pieces and four 6-hole, corner pieces. Insert a green peg into a hole (marking the start of the round) and then put pink pegs into every other hole going around the loom. See the pictures for details.

Casting on
Do this as you did in Step 2. You should end up with three loops of yarn on each peg.

Knitting stitches
Use the one-over-two stitch technique (as described in Step 2) to knit 20 rounds on the loom.

Binding off and filling with FiberFill
Do this as you did in Step 2. When you cut it off from the ball of yarn, leave a yarn tail that's about twice the length of the circumference of the loom. After you close the "working end" of the hat, invert the hat (so that the "ridges" are on the inside). Take the yarn tail and sew it into the opposite, open end. You'll be using this yarn to close this end too, but before you close it, add some polyester FiberFill. Don't stuff it full of the FiberFill—just fill it enough to give it some shape. Then use the yarn to close off the end of the mushroom (tying off the end of the yarn and tucking it away in the mushroom).

Adding mushroom spots
The 24 AI pieces are the mushroom spots; I made eight spots for each of the three mushrooms. It's difficult to adapt the mooshroom's mushroom spots to a 3D round object, but you can look at the pictures here to see what I did. (You can also look at the mooshroom pictures linked in Step 7 to get other ideas for approaching this.) Basically, I put one spot on each narrow end (where the ball was bound off), just below the center. I then put three spots on the front and back sides of the mushroom. For placing these three spots: On each side, I put a spot at the same height as the two end spots, but centered on its respective side, and I then placed the other two squares around this one. See the pictures for how exactly I did this. Glue on the spots as described in Step 7.

Making additional mushrooms
Be sure to repeat this entire step two more times so you end up with three mushrooms.

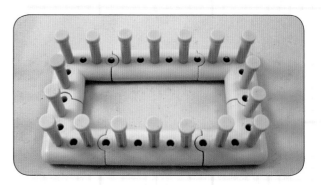

Making the stems

To make stems for the mushrooms I used pieces of a cardboard tube (from a paper towel roll or toilet paper roll). I cut the tube pieces so that they were about 1.6 cm tall. To give it more of a Minecraft feel, I then folded the pieces into square shapes (see the pictures).

Attaching the mushrooms

To attach a mushroom to the body, put glue around both open sides of a cut tube piece, place the piece where you want the mushroom centered on the body, and then center the mushroom on top of this (making sure the spots are oriented correctly). I then put a paperback novel on top of the mushroom for 30+ minutes while it glued. Repeat this process to attach the other two mushrooms. I recommend attaching only one at a time.

Note: Be sure to attach the mushroom to the head before attaching the head to the body, as this is a lot easier to do. Once the mushroom is attached to the head, you can attach the head the same way you did for the legs—just use some yarn and the knitting needle to basically sew the head to the body (making sure it's placed correctly). You will end up sewing the sides of the head closed a little so that you get a nice curve that you can sew onto the curve of the hat (giving the mooshroom a truncated neck). See the pictures here and in the next step for how the mooshroom's head attachment should look.

Step 10: Attaching the Mushrooms

Arranging the mushrooms

Again, refer to pictures of mooshrooms in Step 7 to get an idea of where to place the mushrooms. One mushroom is centered on the head, one is near the middle of the body but off to the right side a little, and the last mushroom is on the far back, off to the left side a little. When you try placing them, make sure they do not bump into each other too much—they should be evenly spaced out.

Step 11: Showing Off Your Awesome Mooshroom Hat!

Once it's done, show off your awesome fungus-ridden hat—great for conventions! Or embarrass a friend by having them wear it in public! Or just sit around the house looking contemplative while wearing it—it's sure to help enhance your critical thinking abilities.

Enderman Hat

Lydia Sedy

(http://www.instructables.com/id/Minecraft-
Enderman-Hat/)

Get into creative mode and make an Enderman Hat! This hat is easy, fun, and definitely a Minecrafter's favorite.

Step 1: Materials
- 1/2 yard of black fleece
- A few inches of white fleece
- A few inches of light purple/pink fleece
- Optional: A Kitty

Step 2: Cutting Everything Out

You can download the pattern in the previous step or freehand draw your own. The most important things are making sure it's wide enough on the bottom edge (mine is 11 inches) and that it's symmetrical. For the eyes, I used graph paper to ensure the measurements are correct. Mine was 4 squares per inch, so the eyes are 3 inches long and 1 inch high.

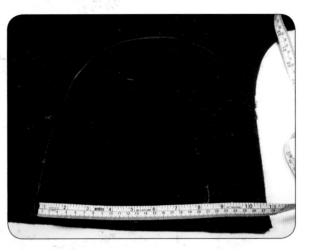

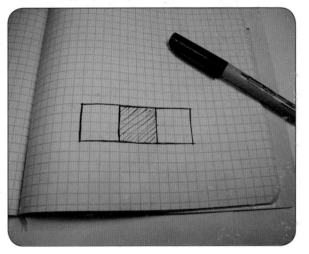

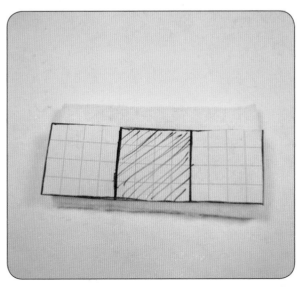

153

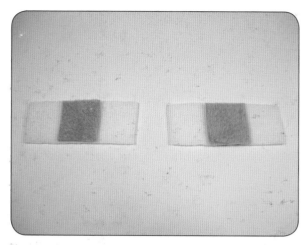

Step 3: Putting Darts in Top of Hat

Take each part of the black pieces and fold them in half, hot dog style, with the right sides in. At the very top, measure two inches down and mark with a pin. About 1/2 inch over from the fold on the top, draw a diagonal line with a piece of chalk down to the pin you marked (first picture). Sew along this line to make a dart, decreasing the size of the top (pictures 2 and 3).

Step 4: Sewing the Hat Together

Take the two black sections and match the darts at the top. Pin in place. Match the sides all around and pin as well. Sew along the entire edge. Optional: You can finish the bottom edge with an overstitch to make it look nicer. This was stitch 7 on my machine.

Step 5: Sew Up the Brim

Keep the hat inside out and try it on. Fold the excess fabric up to your desired length. Using a mirror, pin the brim so you can keep the placement. Be careful not to poke yourself! Once you have the hat off, measure where you pinned and make sure it's the same all the way around the hat, pinning as you go. Sew all the way around. Turn right side out, and you have finished the basic hat! Of course, make sure your kitty approves before you continue.

Step 6: Sew on the Eyes

Place the white eyes where you want them and pin in place. Select a zigzag stitch and sew around the edges. Make sure your curious kitty doesn't get in the way of the needle! Next, place the purple squares in the center and pin in place. Sew around the edges. You have finished your Enderman hat! If you would like to see more of my hats you can visit facebook.com/lydslids.

Creeper Costume

Pete Kumpon

(http://www.instructables.com/id/
Telescoping-Minecraft-Creeper-Costume/)

Minecraft is an obsession in my house. When my 8- and 10-year-old kids aren't playing it, they are sharing the details of the obsidian they just mined, or are drawing up plans for their next creations. So when it came time to choose this year's Halloween costumes, the characters of Minecraft were an easy choice. After carefully considering all of the available characters, including sheep, skeletons, or one of the many skins of Minecraft Steve, my daughter settled on a creeper. I knew this would be a very cool-looking costume—but I wasn't sure how practical it would be. The creeper has a long body with four short legs to support it. Wearing a costume with a body section that extended to her feet would make it near impossible to walk—let alone climb stairs when trick-or-treating. We considered shortening the body so that the feet were closer to her waist. This would improve the mobility, but would definitely look a bit odd. After some brainstorming and multiple design sketches, we finally found the solution to our dilemma: a telescoping lower body! It could be lowered when stationary and then raised up for walking. With a design concept in hand, we set about making our creeper!

Step 1: Materials & Tools
- Cardboard sheets
- Photoshop or similar photo editing software
- Sheetrock screws
- Liquid nails
- Scotch tape
- 3M spray adhesive
- Velcro
- Gorilla Glue
- Scrap foam

Tools you will need:
- Color printer
- Straight edge

- Utility knife
- Xacto knife

Step 2: Get Your Dimensions

I've found that the key to making a great-looking character costume is to have it scaled correctly. Without a creeper action figure (does this even exist?) to measure, we downloaded one of the many papercraft templates that are available online. Papercraft templates are great in that they give you all of the dimensions you need on a single sheet of paper.

Once you've gathered the dimensions, you will need to then determine your scale factor. Since this costume is for my daughter, we took our key scaling dimension off of her. Our scaling dimension was measured from her shoulders to the ground. The thought is that the body portion of the costume is supported by her shoulders, and as a result the shoulders of the creeper costume need to match this height.

The scale factor can then be applied to all of the dimensions from the papercraft template. You are now ready to start cutting cardboard.

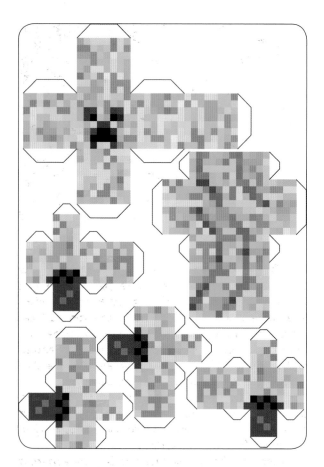

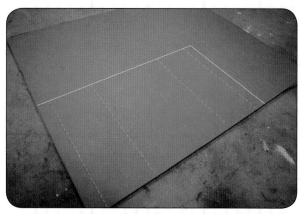

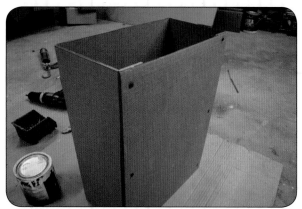

Step 3: Make the Body

The creeper character is essentially made up of rectangular box shapes. This makes cardboard the logical choice of construction material. It's cheap, easy to cut, and easy to fasten together with glue. Our costume was made up of three distinct sections: head, body, and lower body. We started with construction of the body, which is itself constructed from three separate pieces. The front surface and side surfaces were made from a single piece of cardboard with two small flanges—one on each side—for easy attachment of the back surface. We attached the pieces together using liquid nails. Sheet metal screws were used to cinch the pieces together and hold them in place while the glue cured. This provides the added benefit of allowing the partially assembled box to be handled before the glue is dry.

Next the end cap was added. This too had flanges that were used for gluing to the body section. A square-shaped hole was later cut into this end cap to allow my daughter's head to fit through.

Arm holes then need to be added on the side surfaces. Make these oversized to facilitate the process of putting the costume on and taking it off.

Helpful hint: We found that scoring the cardboard before bending allowed for much cleaner folds.

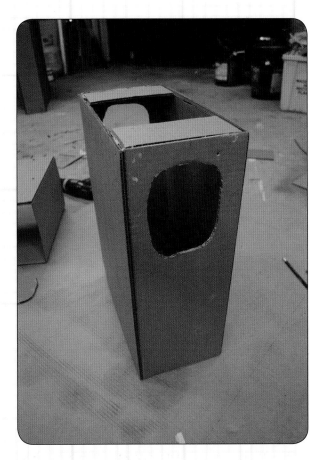

Step 5: Make the Head

The head, which is essentially a cube, was constructed from three separate pieces. The first piece makes up the top of the head and three sides. The three sides fold down from the top surface, which starts to make up the shape of the cube. The edges are secured together with cardboard angles and liquid nails. Sheet metal screws are again used to hold everything together while the glue dries.

The fourth side surface is added and again attached with cardboard angles. If my cardboard sheet were large enough, I would have made this just fold down from the top surface.

Lastly, the bottom surface needs to be added. It has a square hole for a head to poke through. This is attached with cardboard angles.

Step 4: Make the Telescoping Legs

The telescoping section of the costume needs to be snug to the body, but still has to have the clearance to slide freely. We accomplished this by wrapping a strip of cardboard around the body. I placed some cardboard shims between the two sections to ensure there was at least some clearance. With the folds in place, I capped the lower section with a rectangular piece of cardboard.

Legs can now be added to the lower section. The legs are again made from cut and folded cardboard pieces. Flanges are used for attachment to the lower section.

You will have to trim the resulting prints and tape them together. The easiest way to trim the prints is with a sharp Xacto knife and a straight edge. Before attaching your skins, tape all exposed seams on the cardboard with masking tape. This smoothes the transitions and covers the cut edges. Use 3M spray adhesive to attach the skins to your cardboard. Again, tape all of the exposed seams, but do so with Scotch tape this time so that it is not noticeable. As much as I love the 3M adhesive, it does tend to peel back at the edges over time. The tape prevents this.

Step 6: Add the "Skin"

The first step is to make your skins. Our skins were made from images printed on a color laser printer; however, any color printer will do. We used a high-resolution papercraft template as the source image for our creeper (the one you used to get your dimensions may very well work). It took some time to find one that had a high enough resolution to not lose its definition when blown up to sixteen times its size.

Once you settle on your image, open it in Photoshop. Next, open up a blank Photoshop file and set the canvas size to exactly match the dimensions of your surface of interest on the costume. For instance, each side of our head measured 14" x 14", so we set the canvas size to that for all surfaces on the head. Back in the papercraft image, select the surface you wish to enlarge and paste it in the new canvas. Perform a free-transform to stretch it to completely fill the canvas. The file can then be saved to a PDF. You can find PDF templates on the website. These can be scaled to meet the size you need. The body image can be used for all sides of the body with some trimming where needed. The file can then be opened in Adobe and printed to a color printer. Be sure to print it with no scaling (100 percent size). To do this, select: Page Scaling>Tile Large Pages.

Step 7: Assembly

There are two assembly steps:

1. Tethering the lower leg section to the body section: A two-foot length (approximately) of Velcro was used to tether these two sections of the costume together. The Velcro is secured to the lower leg section on the inside, near the bottom. It is attached to the body section on the inside, just beneath the arm hole. We secured the Velcro with Gorilla Glue.

Be sure to leave a short length of Velcro at the top. This will be used to hold up the lower leg section of the costume when the wearer needs to have it up for walking. The Velcro mates with a small piece on the outside of the costume, mounted towards the top of the lower leg section. This may sound a bit confusing, but it makes a lot more sense in the photos.

Tether both sides of the costume to evenly support the weight of the lower leg section.

2. Attaching the head: We attached the head with 2" strips of Velcro. This allowed for easy removal of the head (as required to eat candy during the various Halloween festivities). The Velcro was bonded to the cardboard with Gorilla Glue.

Step 8: Finishing Touches

Almost done!

Eye-hole

Cut a hole in the head so that the wearer can see out of it. We cut along the pixel borders to keep it as clean as possible.

Shoulder pads

Foam was also added under the top surface of the body to prevent the cardboard from digging into my daughter's shoulders. This significantly improved the comfort of the costume.

Enhancements and other ideas:

- Camouflage the eye-hole: black screen or nylon stocking could be mounted to the inside of the head to hide the viewing cut-out.

Steve Costume
Pete Kumpon
(http://www.instructables.com/id/Minecraft-Steve-Costume/)

For years we have been trying to convince our kids that Halloween is all about making your costumes, not buying them. Sadly, this has fallen on deaf ears year after year after year. Our vision of what would be awesome and their vision of what would be awesome has never aligned—until now! Thank you, Minecraft! Our kids, like millions of others around the world, are obsessed with all things Minecraft. While I'm not much into gaming myself, I can definitely appreciate the virtues of this game—namely the simplicity and open-ended creativity that it offers. The simplicity in particular is what made this a logical choice for this year's costumes. The pixelated, blocky look of all of the characters make them perfect for construction out of cardboard—which happens to be free and plentiful. After careful consideration of all the possible characters and skins, my son settled on "Minecraft Steve." He wanted to make it as recognizable as possible to the most number of people. Our primary goals for the costume were (1) to make it as close to the actual game character as possible and (2) to allow for the mobility that will be required during Trick-or-Treating. After two weeks, 10 sheets of cardboard, and many late nights, it's safe to say that the results exceeded our expectations.

Step 1: Materials & Tools
- Cardboard sheets
- Photoshop (or similar photo editing software)
- Sheetrock screws
- Liquid nails
- Tape—both masking and Scotch
- 3M spray adhesive
- Velcro
- Gorilla Glue
- Scrap foam (like the kind used to package computers or appliances)
- Color printer
- Straight edge
- Utility knife
- Xacto knife (with lots of replacement blades)
- Screw gun/cordless drill

Step 2: Gather Your Source Images

I've found that one of the keys to making a great costume is to have it scaled correctly. I've seen lots of pictures of Minecraft costumes where the head is too small compared to the body, or the arms are too large compared to the body and head. These were most likely made with pre-existing cardboard boxes. To make ours truly to scale, we were going to need to make our own boxes. And to do that required a complete set of dimensions.

The problem with Minecraft Steve is that there really aren't any action figures to measure (at least not in my house). There are, however, hundreds of papercraft templates out there on the web. The first thing you need to do is to search for a high-resolution template. This will give you every dimension you will need for every component of the body. It will also serve to provide the "skins" for your boxes. . . but more about that later.

Once you've gathered the dimensions, you will need to then determine your scale factor. Since this costume is for my son, we took our key scaling dimension off of him. Our scaling dimension was measured from his shoulders to the ground. The thought is that the body portion of the costume is supported by his shoulders, and as a result the shoulders of Minecraft Steve need to match this height.

The scale factor can then be applied to all of the dimensions from the papercraft template. You are now ready to start cutting cardboard.

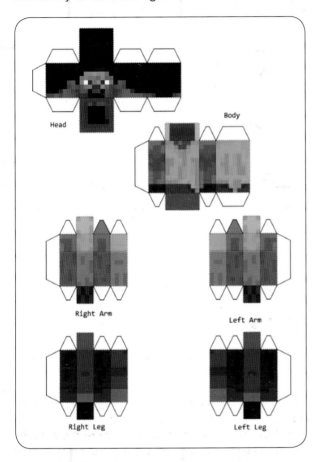

Step 3: Make the Body

The rectangular box-shape of the body was constructed from three separate pieces. The front surface and side surfaces were made from a single piece of cardboard with two small flanges—one on each side—for easy attachment of the back surface. We attached the pieces together using liquid nails. Sheet metal screws were used to cinch the pieces together and hold them in place while the glue cured. This provides the added benefit of allowing the partially assembled box to be handled before the glue is dry.

Next, the end cap was added. This too had flanges that were used for gluing to the body section. A square-shaped hole was later cut into this end cap to allow my son's head to fit through.

Arm holes then need to be added on the side surfaces. Make these oversized to facilitate the process of putting the costume on and taking it off.

Tip: Score the cardboard before bending to allow for much cleaner folds.

Step 4: Make the Head

The head, which is essentially a cube, was constructed from three separate pieces. The first piece makes up the top of the head and three sides. The three sides fold down from the top surface, which starts to make up the shape of the cube. The edges are secured together with cardboard angles and liquid nails. Sheet metal screws are again used to hold everything together while the glue dries.

The fourth side surface is added and again attached with cardboard angles. If my cardboard sheet were large enough, I would have made this just fold down from the top surface.

Finally, the bottom surface needs to be added. It has a square hole for a head to poke through. This is attached with cardboard angles.

Step 5: Make the Arms

The arms are essentially rectangular boxes that are capped on one end. Measure, cut, and fold your cardboard to form the box section. The cap piece is made from a flat piece with two flanges. We experimented with some different ways to configure the end where your arm fits into and found the most comfortable design was to leave that end open and add a large "D"-shaped cutout. A round hole was then added at the "hand" end to allow for holding a pickaxe or sword.

Step 6: Add Your Skins

The first step is to make your skins. As previously mentioned, we used a high resolution papercraft template as the source image for our Minecraft Steve. It took some time to find one that had a high enough resolution to not lose its definition when blown up to eighteen times its size.

Once you settle on your image, open it in Photoshop. Next, open up a blank Photoshop file and set the canvas size to exactly match the dimensions of your surface of interest on the costume. For instance, each side of our head measured 16.25 x 16.25", so we set the canvas size to that for all surfaces on the head.

Back in the papercraft image, select the surface you wish to enlarge and paste it in the new canvas. Perform a free-transform to stretch it to completely fill the canvas. The file can then be saved to a .pdf. Keep in mind that these were sized to fit a 10 year old. They are of a high resolution, so you could stretch them to whatever scale you need. The file can then be opened in Adobe and printed to a color printer. Be sure to print it with no scaling (100 percent size). To do this, select: Page Scaling>Tile Large Pages. You will have to trim the resulting prints and tape them together. The easiest way to trim the prints is with a sharp Xacto knife and a straight edge.

Before attaching your skins, tape all exposed seams on the cardboard with masking tape. This smooths the transitions and covers the cut edges. Use 3M spray adhesive to attach the skins to your cardboard. Again, tape all of the exposed seams, but do so with Scotch tape this time so that it is not noticeable. As much as I love the 3M adhesive, it does tend to peel back at the edges over time. The tape prevents this.

163

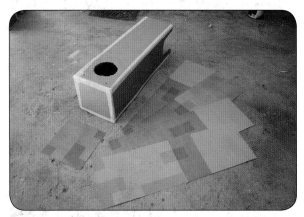

Step 7: Finishing Touches

With the heavy construction done, it's time for some final details.

Velcro the head

The head, which ends up being pretty large relative to the body, needs to be secured in place to prevent it from inadvertently flopping off. We used some strips of 2" Velcro and Gorilla - glued them to the body and underside of the head.

Eye-hole

Next, cut a hole in the head so that the wearer can see out of it. We cut along the pixel borders to keep it as clean as possible.

Hand grips

Since the costume arm is much larger than the wearer's arm, we needed to add a feature that could be grabbed with your hand to keep the arm from falling off. We cut a "U"-shaped piece of Styrofoam and glued it near the circular hole with liquid nails. This worked really well, and allows for maximum flexibility when defending yourself against creepers or mining for cobblestone.

Shoulder pads

Foam was also added under the top surface of the body to prevent the cardboard from digging into my son's shoulders. This significantly improved the comfort of the costume.

Other additions and ideas

Pickaxe: How can you dress up as Minecraft Steve and not have a pickaxe? Go here for some quick and easy instructions: http://www.instructables.com/id/Minecraft-Pickaxe-5-and-45-minutes/

Arch-nemesis: Does your Minecraft Steve need a mortal enemy? Build a Creeper Costume: http://www.instructables.com/id/Telescoping-Minecraft-Creeper-Costume/

Legs: We discussed adding legs to the costume, but ultimately decided that it would making climbing stairs nearly impossible. This would have put a serious damper on trick-or-treating.